"What a helpful book. Clear: it focuses us on Jesus. Wise: it reminds us that his work on the cross is sufficient. Rewarding: it offers reflections and prayers that reveal the treasures of John's Gospel. A great resource to use through Lent. Buy it for yourself and give one to a friend."

REV'D JAMES LAWRENCE, *Leadership Principal, CPAS*

"Lent is usually a time for fasting, but this new book by Tim Chester will help you to enjoy it as a time of feasting on God's word. Short yet profound daily readings in John's Gospel, which are deeply devotional without sacrificing exegetic rigour, will help you to meet Jesus and to gaze on his glory as revealed by his word and actions, and especially through the cross and resurrection. Suggested prayers and mediations will help you to apply these truths to your heart, strengthening your faith and love for Christ. Although structured especially for use in Lent, this book would be spiritually profitable for daily readings at any time of year."

JOHN STEVENS, *National Director, Fellowship of Independent Evangelical Churches*

"*The Glory of the Cross* is a brilliant resource. Tim writes beautifully, accessibly and concisely. As well as shedding light on the text of John's Gospel, he adds a rich diversity of comments and prayers from the full range of Christian history. The chapters are rich enough for anyone to benefit from, but short enough for anyone to manage (a rare balance!). While the idea of 47 readings for "Lent" may not immediately resonate with many of us, this book provides a marvellous way to work through John's Gospel in the run-up to Easter (or actually, at any time). I hope this book is widely used, for if it is, the benefit to God's people as we chew over John's Gospel will be significant."

GARY MILLAR, Principal, *Queensland Theological College*

"A great read for those for whom Easter has, dare I say it, got a bit perfunctory. They know their sin, they know the story, they know the cross. Is that you? Well, I pray you'll have the courage and energy to go on this journey through John's Gospel and let your blindness be exposed. I found it profoundly enlightening and refreshing."

RICO TICE, *Senior Minister (Evangelism), All Souls Langham Place and founder of Christianity Explored Ministries*

"So clearly written and heart-warming, accompanied by a judicious sprinkling of quotes from hymn-writers and luminaries of the Christian church down the centuries, united in finding glory in the cross because of the One who died on it for us. What a splendid resource for Lent!"

DR STEVE BRADY, *Moorlands College, UK*

"Reading *The Glory of the Cross* made me sad and glad! The sadness was the realisation of how hard I find it to see the real glory of Jesus because I am so self-centred. The gladness was that through John's Gospel I was constantly reminded of how wonderful Christ is. This book will clarify the heart of Easter: our fallibility and Christ's magnificent strength to save."

GRAHAM DANIELS, *General Director, Christians in Sport*

"I would want a good supply of these Lenten readings to be on our bookstall right through the year. So often books of readings are cheesy, shallow, frothy and self-centred. These three-page readings however are honouring to Christ, careful with the text, perceptive and edifying. You can give this book to a seeker, new Christian or long-time disciple. Tim Chester takes sections of John's Gospel and shows us the majesty and mercy of Jesus, giving us a great resource."

SIMON MANCHESTER, *Senior Minister, St Thomas' Anglican Church, Sydney*

TIM CHESTER

The Glory of the Cross

Reflections for Lent from the Gospel of John

thegoodbook
COMPANY

The Glory of the Cross
© Tim Chester/The Good Book Company, 2018. Reprinted 2018.

Published by:
The Good Book Company

Tel (UK): 0333 123 0880
Tel (US): 866 244 2165
Email (UK): info@thegoodbook.co.uk
Email (US): info@thegoodbook.com

Websites:
UK: www.thegoodbook.co.uk
North America: www.thegoodbook.com
Australia: www.thegoodbook.com.au
New Zealand: www.thegoodbook.co.nz

ISBN: 9781784982560 | Printed in the UK

Design by André Parker

CONTENTS

INTRODUCTION

What do you see when you look at the cross?

What do you see when you look at the cross? If you had been there on that first Good Friday, you would have seen a man, grimacing in pain, covered in blood and sweat, being executed alongside two criminals. It would have been an appalling spectacle.

What would you have made of Jesus? If you were a passer-by, then you would have assumed Jesus was another criminal perhaps, or a political agitator who had fallen foul of Roman justice. If you had known anything of his story—if you knew he had been a roaming preacher—then you might have concluded he was a fraud. All that talk of the coming of God's kingdom had ended here along with his life. Or maybe, like many people today, you would have seen a good man whose noble ideas had brutally hit the buffers of real life. All that talk of love was captivating while it lasted. But it couldn't last. Of course it couldn't. The message of Jesus is a pleasant diversion for children and dreamers, but makes no sense in the real world.

And yet what the church sees when it looks at the crucified Jesus is the Son of God and the Saviour of the world. How is that possible?

That's what John invites us to explore this Easter. He beckons us to look at Jesus and see the very glory of God. John says as much at the beginning of his Gospel: "The Word became flesh and made his dwelling among us. We have seen his glory, the glory of the one and only Son, who came from the Father, full of grace and truth" (1 v 14).

But seeing the glory of God in the person of Jesus is not straightforward. For one thing, whatever you think glory looks like, it doesn't look like the battered and bloodied man we see on Good Friday. Glory is certainly not what comes to mind as we look at the cross. Yet John is clear. The cross is not a glitch en route to Christ's true glory. The cross is Christ's glory.

But John also keeps alerting us to the fact that our human pride will distort what we see. Instead, he invites us to leave our self-centred preoccupations behind so we can recognise and embrace the true Jesus.

Many of us know that Easter is supposed to be the high point of the church calendar. We want it to *feel* glorious—but instead it comes and goes and passes us by. So over the next 47 days, we'll journey through John's Gospel to the foot of the cross. Each week we'll explore one key episode from Jesus' earthly ministry—his teaching, miracles, death and resurrection. The Sunday reading will give you the opportunity to take in the big sweep of the Bible passage; then from Monday to Saturday we will slow down to reflect more deeply.

My hope and prayer is that you will reach Easter Sunday having been thrilled by who Jesus is and what he has done for you—amazed afresh at the glory of the cross.

THE BEGINNING OF LENT

Seeing the Kingdom of God

ASH WEDNESDAY

John 3 v 1-3, 19-21

"What time is it?" I asked. "The meeting's cancelled," my friend replied. It wasn't really an answer to the question I'd asked! Yet I was satisfied because my friend had rightly guessed the reason behind my question and cut straight to the point.

Something like this is going on in this exchange between Jesus and Nicodemus. John 3 might seem a peculiar place to start Lent, but it's here that Jesus first speaks of his death and what it will achieve.

Yet at first, Jesus' response doesn't seem to connect with what Nicodemus has just said. Nicodemus says, "Rabbi, we know that you are a teacher who has come from God". And Jesus replies, "Very truly I tell you, no one can see the kingdom of God unless they are born again" (v 2-3).

But there's a subtext to Nicodemus' words. The Jews were expecting God's Messiah, his promised Saviour-King. They were looking for God's King to come to defeat God's enemies and re-establish God's kingdom over Israel. So when Nicodemus says, "We know that you are … from God", he's really asking, *Are you the One who is from God? Are you the messianic King? Are you about to establish God's kingdom?*

Jesus responds by saying people can't recognise God's King—or see God's kingdom—unless they're born again. Jesus can't engage with Nicodemus' unspoken question unless Nicodemus becomes a changed man.

We like to think of ourselves as modern people, people of reason, impartially evaluating the evidence. But the reality is we're not neutral observers and we're not impartial. We're firmly on one side—and it's the dark side.

Think about when this conversation takes place. Nicodemus comes to Jesus at night because he fears exposure (v 2). Nicodemus meets Jesus in the dark and then asks why he can't see! Nicodemus is himself a picture of the answer to his question.

"Light has come into the world," says verse 19. It's a reference to Jesus himself (1 v 9). Jesus has come, but we've chosen darkness instead of light because we're already biased against Jesus. There are two issues.

First, our deeds are evil (3 v 19). We love sin and we don't want to stop. We don't want to submit to God. In other words, we don't want Jesus as our King.

Second, we fear exposure (v 20). We're too proud to acknowledge that we need Jesus. In other words, we don't want Jesus as our Saviour.

And so we're deeply invested in rejecting Jesus. We come up with all sorts of reasons to reject him as our King and Saviour.

We're all like Nicodemus. We prefer darkness to light. We fear exposure. Underlying all our reasons for not knowing God is the fact that we won't admit our need and we won't submit our lives. And so we need God's Spirit to recognise God's King, because we're hiding from him.

Ash Wednesday is traditionally a day for confession and repentance. Take the opportunity to confess your failure to admit your need and submit your life. Leave behind the shame and guilt and evil—and take a step into the warmth of Christ's light.

Pray
Almighty and everlasting God,
who hatest nothing that thou hast made,
and dost forgive the sins of all them that are penitent:
Create and make in us new and contrite hearts,
that we worthily lamenting our sins,
and acknowledging our wretchedness,
may obtain of thee, the God of all mercy,
perfect remission and forgiveness;
through Jesus Christ our Lord. Amen.

The Book of Common Prayer
(Collect for Ash Wednesday)

THURSDAY

John 3 v 3-13

I wove through the room, looking at name badges. I was supposed to be meeting someone called Robin, but I couldn't see him anywhere. Then a young woman introduced herself. Robin had been there all along, but I couldn't find her because I was expecting a man.

What did Nicodemus expect to see? He *expected* to see a king who would defeat the Romans and restore Jewish rule in Jerusalem. He expected a court, a throne, a palace, an army. He expected all the pomp and power of earthly kings.

And what *did* he see? "Signs" of God at work, yes (v 2). But where was the army, the throne, the glory? In the end, Nicodemus would see the cross (John 19 v 38-39). How could this be God's King?

The kingdom of God was standing in front of Nicodemus. But he couldn't see it because he was looking for something else. And who can blame him? Sometimes it's easy for Christians to forget just how unlikely it is that a pathetic-looking figure on a cross should be God's solution to the problems of the world.

This is why Jesus says we need to be born again (John 3 v 3). God's King confounds all our expectations. He's hidden in plain sight. And, to make matters worse, we're in the dark, hiding from God. So we need an inner transformation in order to recognise God's King.

Nicodemus takes it all very literally and starts trying to imagine a fully grown man re-entering his mother's womb (v 4)—not an image you want to linger on. But Jesus isn't talking about literal births or rebirths (v 5-7, 12). He's talking about spiritual transformation—what's known as "regeneration" (which means "rebirth"). John the Baptist has described Jesus as "the one who will baptise with the Holy Spirit" (1 v 33). John can only make someone wet on the outside. Jesus washes us clean on the inside through the Spirit.

As a Pharisee, Nicodemus assumed he had an inside track on God's kingdom. Nothing could be further from the truth. The self-reliant and self-righteous are the last people to spot the grace of God in action. Our problem cannot be solved by a little bit more moral effort. It's much more fundamental than that. And so is Jesus' solution—spiritual transformation. People (born of the flesh) don't mature into spiritual people through moral or religious improvement (3 v 6). We have to start all over again. Have you been attempting a bit of spiritual DIY lately? Put down your tools, and ask Jesus to do a complete renovation instead.

"What our Lord wants us to present to him," said the 19th-century preacher Oswald Chambers, "is not goodness, nor honesty, nor endeavour, but real, solid sin: that is all he can take from us. And what does he give in exchange for our sin? Real, solid righteousness."

Look at the cross *without* new birth, and you see another victim of Roman violence. Look at the cross as someone who is being remade by the Spirit, and you see God's King winning a victory of love.

Pray

Give me a sight, O Saviour,
Of thy wondrous love to me,
Of the love that brought thee down to earth,
To die on Calvary.

O make me understand it,
Help me to take it in,
What it meant to thee, the holy One,
To bear away my sin.

Then melt my heart, O Saviour,
Bend me, yes, break me down,
Until I own thee Conqueror,
And Lord and Sovereign crown.

Katharine Agnes May Kelly (1869-1942)

FRIDAY
John 3 v 14-16

"The Son of Man must be lifted up." This sounds more promising. After all, "lifted up" is the language of ascension. Monarchs "ascend" to the throne. They're "exalted"—quite literally, for thrones are set on platforms so that, even when the king is seated, he's above everyone else. Members of the royal family are addressed as "Your royal highness". These people are "high".

And God's King will be lifted up too. But when Jesus speaks of being lifted up, he has something very different in mind from the normal pomp of earthly kings. The parallel is not a king on a throne, but a snake on a stick!

Jesus is alluding to a story from the time of Moses (Numbers 21 v 4-9). God had rescued Israel from slavery in Egypt. But in the wilderness they grew impatient with God. "They spoke against God," we're told. So God sent venomous snakes among them. It didn't take long before the people confessed their sin and asked Moses to intercede.

The LORD said to Moses, "Make a snake and put it up on a pole; anyone who is bitten can look at it and

live." So Moses made a bronze snake and put it up on
a pole. Then when anyone was bitten by a snake and
looked at the bronze snake, they lived.

(Numbers 21 v 8-9)

The rebellion of the Israelites was a picture of the rebellion of all humanity. We too "speak against God" and we too face his judgment. But God is gracious. Just as the snake was lifted up, so Jesus says he will be lifted up on the cross.

John elaborates: "For God so loved the world that he gave his one and only Son, that whoever believes in him shall not perish but have eternal life" (John 3 v 16). Here is the meaning of the cross.

- *The cross is God's love for the world.*
- *The cross is God giving his one and only Son.*
- *The cross is God rescuing us from judgment so that we need not perish.*
- *The cross is God making it possible for us to receive eternal life.*

Sin is like the venom of those snakes, infecting all humanity, flowing through our blood, as it were. And the prognosis is death. But at the cross, Christ absorbed the venom of sin in full. He drew it out onto himself, so that he perished and we receive eternal life.

Of course, this story is not the first time we meet a snake in the Bible. Back in the Garden of Eden it was Satan in the form of a serpent who tempted Adam and Eve to rebel against God. But God promised that a son of Adam would crush the serpent and reverse his work.

It was this promise that was paraded on Moses' pole. And it's this promise that was fulfilled at the cross. Jesus absorbed Satan's venom, disarmed his power and set us free.

Perhaps, as you read, you long to know God, but you're wondering whether you've really been born again—doubts creep and clamour inside your mind. Or perhaps you feel as if you're in a losing battle with your sin—you long to change, but you question whether all this Christian stuff is really making a difference.

If that's how you feel, take heart. Those longings may well be a sign of the transforming work of the Spirit. Your focus should not be on the work of the Spirit, which you can't see (v 8). Instead, look to the work of Jesus, which you *can* see—Christ lifted up on the cross, for you (v 14-15).

Meditate

This story is a type of the whole mystery of the incarnation. For the serpent signifies bitter and deadly sin, which was devouring the whole race on the earth ... biting the soul of man and infusing it with the venom of wickedness. And there is no way that we could have escaped being conquered by it, except by the relief that comes only from heaven. The Word of God then was made in the likeness of sinful flesh, "that he might condemn sin in the flesh," as it is written [in Romans 8 v 3].

Cyril of Alexandria (c. 376-444)

SATURDAY

John 3 v 17-18

I was once driving through Pennsylvania when I saw a huge model mushroom. It was raised on a pole so that no passerby could possibly miss Kennett Square, the self-proclaimed "Mushroom Capital of the World". Of course, what happens next depends on whether you like mushrooms.

We lift things up so we can see them. This conversation with Nicodemus started with Jesus saying, "No one can see the kingdom of God unless they are born again". What does the kingdom of God look like? The Jews thought it would look like a blaze of glory, the defeat of God's enemies and the vindication of God's people. But, no, that's not what it really looks like—at least, not yet. First it looks like a man on a cross.

One day the kingdom of God will indeed involve the defeat of God's enemies. The problem is we're all God's enemies. In fact, we're "condemned already" by our unbelief (v 18). But God is gracious. And so first the King comes not to defeat, but *to be defeated* in our place. Verse 17 puts it like this: "For God did not send his Son into the world to condemn the world, but to save the world through him".

That's why in verse 14 Jesus doesn't simply say he *will* be lifted up. He says he *must* be lifted up. Why was the bronze snake lifted up? So that everyone could see it and be healed.

Imagine you're an Israelite, lying in your tent. Your leg is swollen from a snake bite and the venom is attacking your vital organs. Then someone shouts, "The bronze snake is coming!" What happens next all depends on your faith. You might say, "What good is a fake snake? Leave me alone to die." Or you might say, "I trust God's promise, so I'm going to drag my body out to see and live".

In the same way, people are saved from eternal death by looking to the death of Jesus on the cross. Jesus was lifted up publicly so that it would be written into the annals of history that Jesus died on a cross. But what happens next depends on your faith in God's promises. Three times John 3 emphasises that it's faith in Jesus that leads to eternal life:

- *"Everyone who believes may have eternal life in him" (v 15).*
- *"Whoever believes in him shall not perish but have eternal life" (v 16).*
- *"Whoever believes in him is not condemned" (v 18).*

Here's the problem. What do we see when we look at the cross? Humanly speaking, we see a pathetic figure dying in shame and defeat. We don't see God's King. We don't see God's Son. And that's why we need the Spirit to open our eyes—so we see our King and the glory of his love. "The soul is drawn by love," wrote the 4th-century bishop Augustine. "Not necessity but pleasure; not obligation but delight" (Tractates on the Gospel of John 26.4). Marvel for a moment that this is the means God has chosen!

How does *this passage* end? "Whoever lives by the truth comes into the light, so that it may be seen plainly that what they have done has been done in the sight of God" (v 21).

And how does *this story* end? With a changed life. In John 7 v 50-51 Nicodemus publicly defends Jesus, even though he gets mocked as a result. And, after the crucifixion, a disciple named Joseph gets permission to bury Jesus, and is "accompanied by Nicodemus, the man who earlier had visited Jesus at night" (19 v 39). Nicodemus, the man who visited Jesus in secret, goes public. He risks all to bury Jesus. He is a man made new. He has been born again.

Will you, like Nicodemus, take a risk to honour Jesus today?

Pray

Lord, I was blind; I could not see
In thy marred visage any grace,
But now the beauty of thy face
In radiant vision dawns on me.

Lord, I was deaf; I could not hear
The thrilling music of thy voice;
But now I hear thee and rejoice,
And all thine uttered words are dear!

Lord, I was dumb; I could not speak
The grace and glory of thy name;
But now, as touched with living flame,
My lips thine eager praises wake.

William Tidd Matson (1833-1899)

THE FIRST WEEK OF LENT

Seeing the Bread of Life

SUNDAY

John 6 v 25-59

When I got home from school as a child, I routinely ate bread. Lots of it. I would take three or four slices at a time, hold them together in a big wodge and munch my way through. I could easily work my way through half a loaf. I was a growing boy! My mum didn't mind, because the alternative was having me plunder whatever else I could find in the kitchen cupboards.

In many cultures of the world, bread is the staple food. Nothing matters more than bread. For no one goes hungry when bread is available.

Jesus describes himself as "the bread of life". What does this mean? What hunger does he fill? What nutrients does he give? And how on earth do you eat heavenly bread?

Pray

Pray through the reading by taking a verse or two at a time. Each time identify…
- *something to praise God for*
  - *something to confess*
- *something to turn into a request*

MONDAY

John 6 v 1-21

A man walks into a bar, orders a drink and joins the conversation of the regulars. At one point a man shouts out, "No. 7". Everyone laughs. Moments later someone else shouts, "No. 27". More laughter. When an old man shouts, "No. 33" the place erupts. The man asks the barman what's going on. "Ah, you see, we got so used to hearing the same old jokes again and again that we decided to give each one a number—it saves time." So the man decides to give it a go. He shouts out, "No. 10". Nothing. Just an awkward silence. He casts a quizzical look at the barman. The barman shrugs: "It's the way you tell 'em".

John tells two stories in John 6: a story of Jesus miraculously feeding more than 5,000 people and a story of Jesus walking on the lake. But for those who know the history of Israel, John has embedded clues that evoke other stories—stories for which Jesus is the punchline.

After the feeding of the 5,000, the crowd "get" it. "Surely this is the Prophet who is to come into the world," they say (v 14). They can spot that this is a repeat of the time when Moses fed the Israelites with manna from heaven on their journey out of slavery in

Egypt (Exodus 16). They remember the promise of a new Moses-like prophet (Deuteronomy 18 v 18).

Then, on the lake, Jesus says, "It is I; don't be afraid" (John 6 v 20). It's literally "I am". It echoes God's words in Isaiah 43 v 2, 5: "When you pass through the waters, I will be with you … Do not be afraid, for I am with you." And what is Isaiah talking about in Isaiah 43? He's looking ahead to a new exodus out of captivity in Babylon.

Add it all up and what do you get? Jesus is a new Moses leading a new exodus.

And just to make sure you don't miss it, John begins these stories by saying, "The Jewish Passover Festival was near" (John 6 v 4). It's a somewhat random comment, unless John wants to cue us up to see that Jesus is a new Moses leading a new exodus with a new Passover sacrifice.

At the first Passover, Israelite families killed a lamb and daubed its blood on the doorframes of their homes. That night the LORD killed every firstborn child in Egypt. But the LORD passed over the houses daubed with blood and the children inside were spared. Pharaoh was forced to release God's enslaved people.

John uses this story to interpret the death of Jesus. Jesus is going to free us from the slavery of sin and the threat of death by becoming the ultimate Passover Lamb. Under the protection of his blood, we escape God's judgment and are set free to be his people.

John shouts out "Exodus 16", "Deuteronomy 18", "Isaiah 43". And we reply, "Got it". And erupt with praise.

Meditate

Glory, glory everlasting
Be to him who bore the cross,
Who redeemed our souls by tasting
Death, the death deserved by us.
Spread his glory,
Who redeemed his people thus.

While we hear the wondrous story
Of the Saviour's cross and shame,
Sing we, "Everlasting glory
Be to God and to the Lamb."
Saints and angels,
Give ye glory to His name.

Thomas Kelly (1769-1854)

TUESDAY

John 6 v 22-35

We once bought a bread machine. You measured out the flour and water, added yeast and salt, and then switched it on. The machine would knead and bake the ingredients, and then two hours or so later you had fresh, warm bread. Our machine even had a timer, so you could set it so that your bread would be waiting for you in the morning. We used it often for a few months. But gradually the novelty wore off, and it ended up at the back of the cupboard.

As far as the crowds are concerned, Jesus looks as if he could be a perpetual bread machine. That's what makes them so interested in him. "You are looking for me ... because you ... had your fill," says Jesus (v 26).

What are looking for when you come to Jesus? What would make your life full or complete? "How many seek Jesus," Augustine reflected, "for no other objective than to get some kind of temporal benefit! ... Jesus is scarcely sought after for his own sake ... Here too he says, *you seek me for something else; seek me for my own sake.*" (Tractates on the Gospel of John 25.10)

Jesus says there is something more important than bread. Bread does matter, because we need food to live, and bread is our staple food. Bread equals life. So what could matter more than life? Answer: eternal life. "Do not work for food that spoils," says Jesus, "but for food that endures to eternal life" (v 27).

The crowd respond by asking for a sign. *What will you do? Why not do a Moses—and give us some bread?!* They delve into God's word, but only so they can bring the conversation back round to their favourite theme—free bread from the magic bread machine.

So Jesus makes it personal. They are so focused on the gift that they've lost sight of the true Giver. "It is my Father who gives you the true bread from heaven" (v 32). What really counts is your relationship with God.

And what's the gift? Jesus himself. "I am the bread of life" (v 35). In other words, it's knowing God in Christ that truly satisfies. "Whoever comes to me will never go hungry, and whoever believes in me will never be thirsty" (v 35).

We all have a deep-seated longing for God. It is God who completes us because we were made for him. But in our rebellion against him, we look for that fulfilment anywhere and everywhere but in God. But anything else turns out to be "food that spoils" (v 27).

Sometimes we even go to God in the hope that he will give us our preferred God-substitute. What are you looking for when you come to Jesus? Health, prosperity, a spouse, a new job, a happy family? There's nothing wrong with wanting these things, just as there's nothing wrong with wanting bread. But there is something wrong when you can't see past these thing to Jesus himself. If they matter more than Jesus, then they've become idols. How can you tell? If Jesus is not enough to make you content—if you need *Jesus plus*—then something is wrong. It's time to come back to the Bread of Life and feast on him again.

Meditate

Take delight in the LORD,
and he will give you the desires of your heart.

Psalm 37 v 4

Whom have I in heaven but you?
And earth has nothing I desire besides you.

Psalm 73 v 25

WEDNESDAY

John 6 v 35-40, 44

H ere's my story as told by me.

Once when I was in my 20s I was chatting to my parents. "I think I became a Christian when I was four," I told them. "I remember talking with Mum one Sunday at bedtime. And then she got Dad and we all prayed together around my bed." "It's funny you should say that," they replied, "because that's when we think you became a Christian."

It won't come as a surprise to learn that the four-year-old me had not been involved in sex, drugs and rock 'n' roll. My life was not turned around, aged four—at least, not in ways I can remember. So when I was ten or eleven I had a long period when I lacked assurance. Was I really saved? Had I repented enough? It was a dark and intense time because I knew that my eternal future was at stake. I can even remember thinking it would have been better not to have been born than face this agony of doubt.

Then one Sunday evening my father was preaching at another church and I went with him. He spoke on John 6. I remember hearing Jesus' words, "Whoever comes to me I will never drive away" (v 37). "I've come to Jesus," I thought, "and he promises not to send me away." Ever since, whenever doubts have resurfaced in my mind, I've gone back to this promise.

Faith is not like saving up your money. It's not something you gradually accumulate until you have enough to make the purchase. Faith is to *entrust yourself*—all that matters is that what you entrust yourself *to* is trustworthy. The crowd ask what "works" (plural) God requires (v 28). What great feats must we perform? But God only requires one "work" and it's not really a "work" at all—it's to receive the work Jesus has done. "The work of God is this: to believe in the one he has sent" (v 29).

As a boy sitting in that pew, I remember this thought dawning on me: "The quality of my faith or repentance is not what counts. What counts is the one to whom we come. And I've come to Jesus."

And here's my story as told by Jesus: "All those the Father gives me will come to me ... No one can come to me unless the Father who sent me draws them" (v 37, 44).

Why did the four-year-old me turn to God? Why did the eleven-year-old me trust the promise of Jesus? Because the Father had given me to Jesus. Because the Father was drawing me to Jesus.

I don't remember accompanying my father on any other occasion when he was preaching elsewhere. So why was I with him this particular time? So that I could hear the promise of Jesus. And I must have read John 6 many times before that night. So why was this night different? Because the Father was drawing me to Jesus.

This truth, too, is a great comfort to me whenever I feel uncertain—and as you reflect on your own story, it can be a great comfort to you too. Ultimately, your salvation doesn't rest on your decision, but on God's decision. Left to yourself, your decision might change. After all, there are all sorts of things we change our minds about. For the first twenty years of my life I hated tea. Now I drink it all the time. Could I change my mind about Jesus in the same way? I don't think so—because it's the Father who has drawn me to Jesus. And he never changes his mind.

And if the Father has drawn you to Jesus, he will never change his mind about you either. Let this truth fill you with comfort and inspire you with confidence.

Pray

Just as I am, without one plea,
But that thy blood was shed for me,
And that thou bidst me come to thee,
O Lamb of God, I come.

Just as I am, though tossed about
With many a conflict, many a doubt,
Fightings and fears within, without,
O Lamb of God, I come.

Charlotte Elliott (1789-1871)

THURSDAY

John 6 v 41-50

In practice most of us operate with a ranking of sin. There are bad sins and not-so-bad sins. Just think about which of your sins you're willing to talk about in public and which you keep secret. And it's true that some sins impact other people more than other sins. I'd rather have a self-righteous hypocrite living next door than a violent psychopath. At least self-righteous people put the bins out. But in God's eyes, sin is sin. Every sin is an act of doubt against his word and an act of defiance against his rule.

Grumbling, I expect, is in most people's not-so-bad category. But that's not how God sees it. From God's perspective, grumbling is a declaration that God is a bad King who doesn't run the world very well, and a bad Father who doesn't care for his children properly. It's a way of saying, "I could do a better job than God".

The story of Moses giving manna to Israel in the wilderness hangs in the background of this conversation between Jesus and the crowd. It's a story of God's generous provision. But it's also a story of Israel's persistent grumbling. "In the desert the whole community grumbled against Moses and Aaron" (Exodus 16 v 2). But Moses knew what lay behind their complaints: "You are not grumbling against us, but against the Lord" (Exodus 16 v 8). Indeed, the story of manna is the second of three stories of Israel's grumbles (see also Exodus 15 v 22-27 and 17 v 1-7).

Now the Jews listening to Jesus are at it again. "At this the Jews there began to grumble about him" (John 6 v 41).

In Exodus 17 the three grumbling stories come to a climax when God convenes a trial. God himself is in the dock along with the people. This is the case of God versus humanity. God "stands" before a rock and the elders of the people stand on the opposite side of Moses. Moses stands in the middle and holds the staff which brought judgment against Egypt. He's the one who will pass judgment.

We can all see who's guilty and who's innocent. Anyone who has ever grumbled deserves to be condemned and God deserves to be vindicated. "I will rain down bread from heaven for you," God had said in Exodus 16 v 4, "and in the morning you will see the glory of the Lord" (v 7). The evidence of God's generosity lay scattered across the ground every morning—just as the evidence of God's generosity is all around us each day.

Jesus, at it were, reconvenes that trial when he says, "Stop grumbling" (John 6 v 43). On trial are the religious leaders versus Jesus. At stake is whether Jesus really is the bread of life from heaven. For now, we'll have to wait for the verdict. That will come when God raises Jesus from the dead. The final proof that Jesus is the bread of life will come when he gives eternal life to those who "eat" him.

But there was a dramatic twist in the trial of Exodus 17. At its climax God declared, "Strike the rock"—the place where God was standing. The rod of judgment came down on God instead of the people, on the innocent instead of the guilty. As a result, water gushed from the rock to quench the thirst of God's people. "That rock was Christ," says Paul in 1 Corinthians 10 v 4. Christ died in our place so that grumbling might be met with grace. We receive life through the cross—as Jesus is about to explain. And as he died, water flowed from his wounded side to quench our spiritual thirst (John 19 v 34).

The antidote for grumbling is gratitude. What are the signs of God's generosity that lie scattered around you today? Give thanks for each one. And the ultimate sign of God's generosity is the cross, for it was there that he gave his own Son for us. Give thanks for him.

Pray

Lord of all mercy and goodness,
suffer us not by any ingratitude
or hardness of heart
to forget the wonderful benefits
that thou hast bestowed upon us
this and every day;
but grant that we may be mindful
all the days of our life
of the incomparable gifts
which thou ever givest us
through Jesus Christ our Lord.

Early Scottish prayer

FRIDAY

John 6 v 51

We sometimes say things like, "I'm in a dead-end job". "It's squeezing the life out of me." "He'll be the death of me." These are all signs that life is not what it's meant to be. Life is touched by death.

We're all dying physically. I hope that as you read this you're in the best of health. But death comes to us all. And the aches and pains, the grey hairs and failing energy, are reminders that it's on its way.

And we're all dead spiritually. Without Christ, we're cut off from the One who gives life. We're dead to God. We can't hear his voice or know his presence. Sin has the better of us and we're powerless to do anything about it.

But just as bread gives life, so Jesus gives life. Just as we need to eat in order to live, so by "eating" Jesus, the spiritual bread of life, we live.

But there's also a big difference. We eat bread, but tomorrow we're hungry again. I had toast for breakfast this morning, and the chances are I'll have it again tomorrow. I can't say, "I don't need to eat—I did that yesterday".

But the bread which Jesus gives satisfies not just for a day, but for ever. This spiritual food brings life—life eternal. This is the big difference between manna and

Jesus. "Your ancestors ate manna and died," says Jesus, "but whoever feeds on this bread will live for ever" (v 58). This bread, said Ignatius of Antioch in the first century, is the "medicine of immortality and the antidote against death" (Letter to the Ephesians).

One day everyone's physical bodies will die—that's the one great inescapable fact of life (that, and taxes). But Jesus promises to give eternal life. How can that be true when Christians end up dead like everyone else? The answer is that Jesus promises that on the last day he will raise his people from the dead to eternal life:

- *"I shall lose none of all those he has given me, but raise them up at the last day" (v 39).*
- *"I will raise them up at the last day" (v 44).*
- *"Whoever eats my flesh and drinks my blood has eternal life, and I will raise them up at the last day" (v 54).*

When a Christian dies, their soul—their essential personality—goes to be with God. But their body is buried or cremated. It wastes away. But Jesus promises that on the last day he will raise it up again. You'll have a new body—just like Jesus himself when he was raised from the dead on that first Easter Day.

Jesus describes himself as "living bread" (v 51). That's because *he himself* is the bread. That's because the life of "the living Father" is in Jesus (v 57). That's because Jesus will live again after death. And that's because through his resurrection, he will become *life-giving bread*.

But notice, too, that Jesus gives life by giving his own life. "This bread is my flesh, which I will give for the life of the world" (v 51). The more this conversation pro-gresses, the closer it gets to Easter. We are dying and he is the living One. But Jesus died so that we might live.

Does it feel as if your Christian life lacks life? Has your fizz gone flat? The Spanish monk John of the Cross wrote, "My spirit is dry within me because it forgets to feed on thee". Feed on Christ and feel full—today, tomorrow, and for eternity.

Pray

Guide me, O thou great Jehovah,
Pilgrim through this barren land.
I am weak, but thou art mighty;
Hold me with thy powerful hand.
Bread of Heaven, Bread of Heaven,
Feed me till I want no more.

William Williams Pantycelyn (1717-1791)

SATURDAY

John 6 v 52-59

To receive the gift of eternal life, Jesus says we must eat his flesh and drink his blood. It's a vivid pic-ture, but what does it mean? After all, it sounds gro-tesque! The Old Testament law prohibited consuming blood or meat with blood in it—so for Jesus' hearers it was doubly grotesque (v 60-61).

Jesus has already told us what it means: "The work of God is this: to believe in the one he has sent" (v 29). We eat through faith in Jesus. But this is much, much more than simply agreeing to some truths about Jesus. Faith ties us to Jesus. It's relational. It involves embracing a real flesh-and-blood person. "Whoever eats my flesh and drinks my blood remains in me, and I in them" (v 56). We ingest Jesus, as it were, so that his life is in us.

So this belief is not just an intellectual assent. The picture of eating and feeding suggests something much more engaged. Imagine you're starving and someone offers fresh, warm, yeasty bread. It would be no good saying, "I believe by eating this bread I will live" without actually then eating it! And it's no good saying, "I think Jesus is the bread of life" unless you actually commit yourself to him, wholeheartedly, in obedience and trust.

At this point, let me hand over to a guest contributor, the 16th-century Reformer John Calvin:

> *There are some who define the eating of Christ's flesh and the drinking of his blood, as, in one word, nothing but to believe in Christ. But it seems to me that Christ meant to teach something more definite, and more elevated, in that noble discourse in which he commends us to the eating of his flesh [John 6 v 26 onwards]. It is that we are made alive by the true partaking of him; and he has therefore designated this partaking by the words "eating" and "drinking", in order that no*

one should think the life that we receive from him is received by mere knowledge. As it is not seeing but the eating of bread that suffices to feed the body, so the soul must truly and deeply become a partaker of Christ that it may be quickened [restored] to spiritual life by his power.

We admit indeed, meanwhile, that this is no other eating than that of faith, as no other can be imagined. But here is the difference between my words and theirs: for them to eat is only to believe; I say that we eat Christ's flesh in believing, because it is made ours by faith, and that this eating is the result and effect of faith. Or if you want it said more clearly, for them eating is faith; for me it seems rather to follow from faith ...

In this way the Lord intended, by calling himself the "bread of life", to teach not only that salvation for us rests on faith in his death and resurrection, but also that, by true partaking of him, his life passes into us and is made ours—just as bread when taken as food imparts vigour [strength] to the body.

(Institutes, 4.17.5)

By this point in Jesus' conversation with the crowd, he is anticipating the Lord's Supper. Calvin says the Lord's Supper doesn't confer anything that is not given through the preaching of the gospel. But it does confer Christ and his benefits in a special way—"more clearly". It's given to nourish our life-giving faith in Christ and our relationship with him. "It remains for all this [the work of Christ] to be applied to us. That is done through the gospel but more clearly through the Sacred Supper, in which he offers himself with all his benefits to us, and we receive him by faith." (Institutes, 4.17.5) So if you take communion at church tomorrow, use it as an opportunity to reflect on something you've been particularly struck by this week, as you've tasted and savoured the Bread of Life.

Meditate

When bread is given as a symbol of Christ's body,
we must at once grasp this comparison:
as bread nourishes, sustains,
and keeps the life of our body,
so Christ's body is the only food to
invigorate and enliven our souls.
When we see wine set forth
as a symbol of blood,
we must reflect on the benefits
which wine imparts to the body,
and so realise that the same are
spiritually imparted to us by Christ's blood.
These benefits are to nourish,
refresh, strengthen, and gladden.

John Calvin (1509-1564)

THE SECOND WEEK OF LENT

Seeing the Good Shepherd

SUNDAY

John 10 v 1-18

Ten years of preparation unravelled in a moment as the doctor gave his diagnosis. Now the lives of my friends were thrown upside-down. They had been willing to follow Jesus to do a dangerous job in a dangerous part of the world. But now there was no choice but to cancel their plans.

I don't know what confusion or turmoil you're facing in your life. Doubtless there's something, or there will be soon.

And when we hit those moments, we can find ourselves asking: *Can Jesus be trusted?* It sometimes seems he hasn't read the script!

John 10 asks whether Jesus is a *good* shepherd. Is Jesus a shepherd we can follow with glad confidence, even when the path takes an unexpected turn?

Pray
Pray through the reading by taking a verse or two at a time. Each time identify...
* *something to praise God for*
* *something to confess*
* *something to turn into a request*

MONDAY

John 9 v 35-41

"I **I** 've made a list of the pros and cons," my friend told me. I was helping him to make a big decision. "I just don't know what to do," he sighed. But as we talked through the list, it turned out he found all the pros persuasive, while the cons were easy to dismiss. Deep down he did know what he wanted to do. Now he was simply finding reasons to justify that decision.

It's a glimpse of what human beings do all the time. We find reasons for doing what we want to do. Our vision gets distorted by our desires.

Right before Jesus describes himself as the Good Shepherd, he heals a man who has been blind since birth (John 9). As the story of his healing unfolds, it becomes clear that Jesus hasn't just healed his *physical* blindness, but also his *spiritual* blindness—as their subsequent conversation demonstrates. The man is enabled to see who Jesus really is. Jesus identifies himself as God's promised King ("the Son of Man") and the once-blind man responds, "Lord, I believe" (9 v 35-38).

Then Jesus comments, "For judgment I have come into this world, so that the blind will see and those who see will become blind" (9 v 39). It's a bit cryptic.

Jesus is saying that those who think they have spiritual insight—the religious *insiders*—fail to recognise who he is. Meanwhile, the people everyone thinks of as *outsiders* can recognise him. And that includes the blind man. The story started with the disciples asking whether it was the man's sin or his parents' sin that caused him to be born blind (9 v 2). In other words, they assumed he was cursed by God—the only question was whose fault that was. But Jesus turns those assumptions upside down—for it's the once-blind man who alone ends the story seeing Jesus for who he really is.

It might appear cryptic to us, but the Pharisees clearly understood the point Jesus was making. "What? Are we blind too?" they respond (9 v 40).

The real issue had nothing to with their retina and optic nerves. Nor was it about mental capacity. The religious leaders weren't stupid—it wasn't an intellectual problem. It was a heart problem. They didn't believe because they didn't want to believe. Their thinking was clouded by their desires. So they found reasons to dismiss Jesus. They didn't want to admit their need for him or submit their lives to him.

Take the opportunity to ask yourself whether selfish desires are clouding your thinking. Are you finding reasons to justify doing what you know deep down you ought not to do? If you've seen who Jesus really is, will you instead admit your need and submit every area of your life to him?

Pray

Almighty and most merciful Father,
we have erred, and strayed from thy ways like lost sheep,
we have followed too much the devices and desires of our own hearts,
we have offended against thy holy laws,
we have left undone those things which we ought to have done,
and we have done those things which we ought not to have done,
and there is no health in us.
But thou, O Lord, have mercy upon us miserable offenders;
spare thou them, O God, which confess their faults,
restore thou them that are penitent,
according to thy promises declared unto mankind
in Christ Jesus our Lord.
And grant, O most merciful Father, for his sake,
that we may hereafter live a godly, righteous, and sober life,
to the glory of thy holy Name. Amen.

The Book of Common Prayer

TUESDAY

John 10 v 1-6

When British people think "shepherd", we think "sheep dog". We love that intimate relationship between man and dog—the whistles and shouts that direct the dog to round up the sheep from the hillside.

For a while it was even prime-time viewing—back in the 1980s 8 million Brits would tune in to watch sheepdog trials on the TV show *One Man and His Dog*.

But "one man and his dog" is not the image that would have been in the minds of Jesus' hearers. In 2011 my wife and I visited the Middle East and saw shepherds walking across the hillside with their flocks following behind them. The intimate relationship that a British shepherd has with his *dog* is the relationship that a Middle-Eastern shepherd has with his *sheep*.

So it's easy to find out who the true shepherd is. The true shepherd is the one with the sheep following him.

It's the same with Jesus. How do we know Jesus is the true shepherd? Because he's the one with the sheep following him. Back in John's Gospel, it's the once-blind man, who has just said to him, "Lord, I believe" and worshipped him (9 v 38).

And today, we're the proof! Every Christian is proof that Jesus is the true shepherd. Jesus is still gathering his sheep. We may not literally hear the sound of his voice. But we hear his call in the gospel message. When the gospel is proclaimed, those who belong to Jesus hear his voice and respond by saying, "I believe".

Perhaps your conversion was very dramatic; perhaps it wasn't. Perhaps it was a moment in time; perhaps it was a lengthy process. But whatever your story, this is what happened. You heard someone talking about Jesus or you read something someone had written—an ordinary human being. But for you, those words were the words of Jesus himself. He addressed you directly. He called you by name. You heard in those words the voice of the true shepherd.

And still Jesus continues to call you by name. Whenever you read the Bible, Jesus is addressing you by name. In the Bible we hear the voice of Christ. Jesus addresses us personally. You can insert your own name into 10 v 3: "He calls _____ by name and leads them." He speaks words of comfort, challenge and reassurance. So don't just read the Bible to gain some new information. Read it, and hear it preached, to hear the voice of Christ, your shepherd.

Or perhaps you're not a Christian. Perhaps Christianity is all very new to you. Or perhaps you've been going to church all your life, but it's never felt personal. Maybe as you read these words, Jesus is calling you. Hear in these words the voice of the true shepherd and say, "Lord, I believe".

Meditate

I heard the voice of Jesus say,
"Come unto me and rest;
Lay down, O weary one, lay down
Your head upon my breast."
I came to Jesus as I was,
Weary and worn and sad;
I found him in a resting place,
And he has made me glad.

Horatius Bonar (1808-1889)

WEDNESDAY

John 10 v 7-9

Y ou're the sole survivor of a plane crash. You're alone in a tropical jungle. What should you do? According to the survival experts, your priorities should be finding food and water, and then building some kind of a shelter.

The basic needs of sheep are not so very different. They need protection from danger and pasture for food.

In verse 7 Jesus changes metaphors. Instead of being "the shepherd", he describes himself as "the gate". But the change of metaphor is not as big as it first appears to 21st-century readers. In the ancient world, sheep would spend the night in a walled enclosure, and the shepherd would lie across the entrance to prevent predators entering. So the shepherd was like a human gate.

The point is that Jesus keeps us safe. That what's Jesus says in verse 9: "I am the gate; whoever enters through me will be saved"—or "kept safe". "They will come in and go out, and find pasture." During the day the shepherd led his flock to good food, and then at night he protected them from danger.

The contrast is with the thief. "The thief comes only to steal and kill and destroy" (v 10). Jesus probably has in mind Ezekiel 34, where God confronted the leaders—or "shepherds"—of Israel who had not cared for the sheep, but cared only for themselves: "You have ruled them harshly and brutally" (Ezekiel 34 v 4). And then God promises:

> *I myself will search for my sheep and look after them ...*
> *I will pasture them on the mountains of Israel ... I will*
> *tend them in a good pasture ... There they will lie down*
> *in good grazing land, and there they will feed in a rich*
> *pasture on the mountains of Israel ... You are my*
> *sheep, the sheep of my pasture, and I am your God,*
> *declares the Sovereign* LORD.
>
> *(Ezekiel 34 v 11, 13-14, 31)*

Did you notice the repetition of the word "pasture"? Jesus picks up on this when he promises that with *him* as the true shepherd, the sheep will "come in and go out, and find pasture" (John 10 v 9).

God promised through Ezekiel, "I will place over them one shepherd, my servant David, and he will tend them; he will tend them and be their shepherd" (34 v 23). When we first meet David in the Bible story—around 500 years before Ezekiel's prophecy—he is "tending the sheep" (1 Samuel 16 v 11). Then God chose him to shepherd the people. So David was the *original* shepherd-king. But Ezekiel was looking forward to the *ultimate* Shepherd-King—the Lord Jesus, who has now come to care for his sheep and lead them to good pasture.

Imagine you're a sheep on a Middle-Eastern hillside. Why do you follow your shepherd? Because you know he'll lead you to good pasture—even though sometimes en route he'll lead you through rocky terrain.

Why do we follow Jesus? Because we know he'll lead us to good pasture. But sometimes the route takes us over rocky ground. How can we trust him? Because, as we'll see tomorrow, he's the shepherd who lays down his life for the sheep. When the circumstances of life confuse you or make you dismayed, look to the cross. That's the great demonstration that Jesus is the good shepherd. That's the guarantee that he will lead us to a place of eternal rest and safety.

What feeds us as we journey is the word of Christ. Good pasture can be found today in the Scriptures, for it's in the Scriptures that we hear the voice of the Shepherd.

Meditate

The King of love my Shepherd is,
Whose goodness faileth never,
I nothing lack if I am his
And he is mine for ever.

Where streams of living water flow
My ransomed soul he leadeth,
And where the verdant pastures grow,
With food celestial feedeth.

Henry Williams Baker (1821-1877)

THURSDAY

John 10 v 10

We're built for pleasure. We find pleasure... pleasurable! We can cope with a bit of deferred gratification. But even deferred gratification has as its goal eventual gratification.

Yet Jesus calls us to humble ourselves and serve others (see, for example, 13 v 14-17). Christians are called to a life of self-denial and sacrifice. There'll be pleasures you forgo, either because you're saying no to temptation or because you're putting others first.

But Jesus is not like one of those false shepherds whose intent is "only to steal and kill and destroy" (10 v 10). Jesus is not going to fleece us. With Jesus it's not take, take, take. It's give, give, give.

There's a strange dynamic at the heart of Christian discipleship: the more you give, the more you gain. This is how Jesus puts it in 12 v 25: "Anyone who loves their life will lose it, while anyone who hates their life in this world will keep it for eternal life". Jesus doesn't call us to a life of loss. He calls us to a full life: "I have come that they may have life, and have it to the full" (10 v 10).

On the one hand we're called to self-denial; on the other hand we're promised life to the full. One person who thought hard about this paradox was Augustine.

Everyone loves their own good, says Augustine, *so why would anyone choose to embrace self-denial?* The key is to discern the right and wrong sort of love.

> *Anyone who loves himself by leaving God out of his life (and leaves God out of his life by loving himself), does not even remain in himself. He actually leaves his self. He goes away into exile from his own heart by taking no notice of what is inside and instead only loving what is outside.* (Sermon 330)

In other words, there's a form of self-love which actually leads to self-alienation. We think we'll be better off without God, but end up dehumanised. We pursue pleasure and end up feeling lost—in "exile from [our] own heart". The pop star Robbie Williams once said in a television interview, "I've got what everybody wants. When I was young and I looked at people like me, I wanted it. But now I've got it all, I'm finding it hard to find any bit of it that I enjoy."

Augustine took the pursuit of money as an example. "By loving money, you end up abandoning yourself." You tell lies to get money. You suck up to people you don't like to promote your career or business. "While looking for money, you have destroyed your soul … You end up valuing other things, which are outside you, more than yourself." We sacrifice ourselves for possessions or prestige. Yet these things lure us away from our true humanity. Fulfilment (life "to the full", as Jesus puts it) is found in knowing God and serving others. So Augustine says:

> *Come back to yourself. But then turn upward when you*
> *have come back to yourself; do not stay in yourself. First*
> *come back to yourself from the things outside you, and*
> *then give yourself back to the one who made you, who*
> *looked for you when you were lost and found you when*
> *you were a runaway.*   *(Sermon 330)*

Is there an area of your life where you have chosen what is comfortable over what is costly? Today, when will you be tempted to put yourself first, ahead of your spouse or child or colleague or neighbour? Come back to yourself; come back to God. For it's only in following Jesus, the Good Shepherd who has served you, that you will have life to the full.

Pray

Lord Jesus, our Saviour, let us now come to thee:
Our hearts are cold;
Lord, warm them with thy selfless love.
Our hearts are sinful;
cleanse them with thy precious blood.
Our hearts are weak;
strengthen them with thy joyous Spirit.
Our hearts are empty;
fill them with thy divine presence.
Lord Jesus, our hearts are thine;
possess them always and only for thyself.

Augustine (354-430)

FRIDAY

John 10 v 11-18

But what's the proof that Jesus won't fleece us—that he's the true shepherd? "The good shepherd lays down his life for his sheep" (v 11). As we saw yesterday, we know it's not all take, take, take with Jesus because he gives, gives, gives his own life for us.

Three times in these verses Jesus says, "The good shepherd lays down his life" or "I lay down my life" (v 11, 15, 17). Why?

First, Jesus lays down his life so that we know he's not self-serving (v 11). The death of Jesus means we can distinguish him from the hired hand. The hired hand is just in it for the money, so when the wolf attacks "he abandons the sheep and runs away" (v 12). It's not worth putting up a fight because he "cares nothing for the sheep" (v 13).

Think of what it is that competes with Christ for your affections. What happens when you let that rival down or fail to live up to the standards it requires? If you live for approval or career or possessions or control or anything else, when you mess up you're left feeling afraid, downcast, bitter. But when you let Christ down, he still loves you. Indeed, he died for you. That's how you know he's the real deal. He's not in it for what he can *get* from you. He's in it for what he can *give* to you.

Second, Jesus lays down his life so that we can share his relationship with the Father: "I am the good shepherd; I know my sheep and my sheep know me—just as the Father knows me and I know the Father—and I lay down my life for the sheep" (v 14-15). Jesus invites us to share his relationship with the Father. What prevents that is God's judgment against our sin. But at the cross Jesus dealt with that judgment. As a result, his relationship with the Father becomes our relationship with the Father. John Calvin says, "[Christ], while he is the true Son, has of himself been given us as a brother that what he has of his own by nature may become ours by benefit of adoption" (Institutes, 3.20.36).

This invitation comes to us in the gospel message. That's why Jesus speaks of "other sheep" who will hear his voice (v 16). He's talking about you! Around the world and across the centuries, people are being invited into the fold.

Third, Jesus lays down his life so we know he cares for us (v 17). The death of Jesus was not the tragic end of a failed life. Events didn't spiral out of control when he entered Jerusalem. He was nobody's victim. His life wasn't taken from him. He laid it down of his own accord (v 18). This is not the first or only reason why the Father loves the Son, but it is one big reason (v 17). And this is how we know he's the good shepherd.

If ever you feel that you have reason to doubt Christ's care—perhaps even this very day—then look to the cross. See there the Good Shepherd, *your* Good Shepherd, laying down his life for you.

Pray

Where do you pasture your flock, O Good Shepherd,
you who carry the whole flock on your shoulders?
Show me the place where there is new-grown grass,
make known to me the water of repose,
lead me out to the nourishing pasture,
call me by name in order that I, I your sheep,
may hear your voice, and by your voice give me eternal life.
Speak to me, you whom my soul loves.
For how shall I not love you, who so loved me
as to lay down your life for the sheep that you shepherd.

Gregory of Nyssa (335-395)

SATURDAY

John 10 v 11-14

I have a friend who's a shepherd. It can be hard work, especially during lambing season. Night and day he's on the job, ensuring the lambs are delivered safely. For at least part of the year, his whole life is given over to caring for the sheep. He's a good shepherd.

But only Jesus is *the* Good Shepherd. His is the voice which is heard in the preaching of the gospel; his is the death that rescues the sheep.

But his leadership is a model for all leadership. Whether it's leadership in politics, business or the home, all leaders are to be good shepherds—and none more so than in the church. It's no accident that church leaders are called "pastors" or "shepherds". "Christ is a unique and true shepherd," said the Swiss Reformer Huldrych Zwingli. "But secondarily, he then deigns by his grace to give this name and office to those whom he sends [to] teach that salvation is found through Christ" (Commentary on John 10.11).

Israel's leaders were meant to care for God's people like shepherds. But, as we've seen, God condemned their shepherding in Ezekiel 34:

> *You eat the curds, clothe yourselves with the wool and*
> *slaughter the choice animals, but you do not take care*
> *of the flock. You have not strengthened the weak or*
> *healed those who are ill or bound up the injured. You*
> *have not brought back the strays or searched for the lost.*
> *You have ruled them harshly and brutally. So they were*
> *scattered because there was no shepherd.*
>
> *(Ezekiel 34 v 3-5)*

Here are leaders who neglect and exploit those under their care while they themselves grow rich. It's not hard to find parallels today in politics, business, the church and the home.

In 1 Peter 5 v 1-3, Peter calls on church leaders to "be shepherds of God's flock that is under your care, watching over them…"

- *"not because you must, but because you are willing"*
- *"not pursuing dishonest gain, but eager to serve"*
- *"not lording it over those entrusted to you, but being examples"*

Leaders are not to be like the hired hands of John 10 v 12 —just doing a job to earn a pay packet. Behind Peter's three warnings linger the bad shepherds of Ezekiel 34. Behind his three exhortations stands the example of the Good Shepherd who lays down his life for the sheep.

Implicit in all Peter says is a reminder that God's people do not belong to human leaders. "Be shepherds of *God's* flock," he says, "not lording it over *those entrusted to you*". Leaders may be shepherds, but Christ is "the Chief Shepherd" (1 Peter 5 v 4). So good leaders shepherd the flock by leading them to the Chief Shepherd, and to the good pastures of his word.

If you're involved in leadership at any level, think through what it means for you to follow the example of the Good Shepherd.

And all of us can help our leaders in this task by being good followers. Hebrews 13 v 17 says, "Have confidence in your leaders and submit to their authority, because they keep watch over you as those who must give an account. Do this so that their work will be a joy, not a burden, for that would be of no benefit to you." How could you respect and encourage your church leader as you meet together as God's people tomorrow?

Pray
Now may the God of peace,
who through the blood of the eternal covenant
brought back from the dead our Lord Jesus,
that great Shepherd of the sheep,
equip you with everything good for doing his will,
and may he work in us what is pleasing to him,
through Jesus Christ, to whom be glory for ever and ever.
Amen.

Hebrews 13 v 20-21

THE THIRD WEEK OF LENT

Seeing the Resurrection and the Life

SUNDAY

John 11 v 17-44

"Time will heal." "She's looking down on us." "He had a good life." "She's joined the angels." What do you say in the face of death?

Jesus meets two grieving sisters in John 11. They greet him with exactly the same phrase, word for word:

> *"Lord," Martha said to Jesus, "if you had been here, my brother would not have died." ... When Mary reached the place where Jesus was and saw him, she fell at his feet and said, "Lord, if you had been here, my brother would not have died."*   *(v 21, 32)*

Same loss, same words. But Jesus responds in a completely different way. He's not coming with a one-size-fits-all response to grief. But he does have something to offer. He comes with hope.

Pray
Pray through the reading by taking a verse or two at a time. Each time identify...
- *something to praise God for*
  - *something to confess*
- *something to turn into a request*

MONDAY

John 11 v 17-25

Human beings can be extremely resilient. Some people remain remarkably positive in the face of adversity. Not always, but often. People talk about beating their cancer. People look forward to bouncing back from difficulties. "We'll pull through," we tell one another. But no one beats death and no one bounces back from the grave. Bereavement can't be fixed.

Martha, though, retains a remarkable degree of faith in the face of death. She's confident that, if Jesus had arrived in time, then he could have healed her brother (v 21). And she remains full of faith after his death. "Even now God will give you whatever you ask," she says (v 22). Her subsequent responses suggest she's not expecting Lazarus to be restored. She's probably just affirming that, despite all that's happened, she still trusts Jesus.

Jesus' reply—"Your brother will rise again"—is somewhat ambiguous. Because we know the story, we sense Jesus is talking about an imminent miracle. But Martha takes it, not unreasonably, as a reference to resurrection on the last day at the end of time. She takes it as a spiritual platitude. Jesus, she thinks, is telling her what we might tell a bereaved relative of a Christian: "They're with the Lord." "You'll meet again in heaven." True enough. But such sentiments can sound trite in the midst of loss.

Martha responds with a tremendous statement of faith: "I know he will rise again in the resurrection at the last day". Martha recognises that nothing can separate us from God's love, not even death.

Yet Jesus takes her beyond this. He gives substance to the platitudes. He moves from *There is resurrection,* to *I am resurrection.* He makes it personal.

Jesus gives the *basis* for belief in the resurrection. And that basis is himself. *He* will raise the dead. He has life in himself.

> *Very truly I tell you, whoever hears my word and believes him who sent me has eternal life and will not be judged but has crossed over from death to life. Very truly I tell you, a time is coming and has now come when the dead will hear the voice of the Son of God and those who hear will live. For as the Father has life in himself, so he has granted the Son also to have life in himself.* (5 v 24-26)

The story of Lazarus is going to be an explanation and demonstration of these words—as we'll see over the course of this week.

But perhaps, today, you carry a grief that can't be fixed. Perhaps your faith feels broken, not buoyant. Perhaps you've had your fill of well-meaning yet empty sentiments. Jesus stands ready to meet you: not a platitude, but a person—a person with the power to cross from death to life.

Meditate

I turned round to see the voice that was speaking to me.
And when I turned I saw seven golden lampstands, and
among the lampstands was someone like a son of man,
dressed in a robe reaching down to his feet
and with a golden sash round his chest.
The hair on his head was white like wool, as white as
snow, and his eyes were like blazing fire.
His feet were like bronze glowing in a furnace,
and his voice was like the sound of rushing waters.
In his right hand he held seven stars, and coming out of
his mouth was a sharp, double-edged sword.
His face was like the sun shining in all its brilliance.
When I saw him, I fell at his feet as though dead.
Then he placed his right hand on me and said:
"Do not be afraid. I am the First and the Last.
I am the Living One; I was dead, and now look,
I am alive for ever and ever!
And I hold the keys of death and Hades."

Revelation 1 v 12-18

TUESDAY

John 11 v 25-26

Once, when I was travelling in India, I saw a truck hit a motorbike. I assume the motorcyclist was killed. I will never know. The bus on which I was travelling carried on in the opposite direction. It's the only time I might have seen someone die. In the West we've become adept at hiding dying and death away out of sight. But we can't hide from it from ever.

Strangely, Jesus says those who believe in him both *will die* and *will never die*:

- *They "will live, even though they die".*
- *"Whoever lives ... will never die."*

Jesus is talking about two types of death and two types of life.

First, Jesus says, "I am the resurrection ... The one who believes in me will live, even though they die" (v 25). Here is a recognition that everyone dies. But Jesus promises life after death. Jesus promises a resurrection that leads to eternal life in a new creation.

This is more than a promise of resurrection alone. The Bible says *everyone*—both believers and unbelievers—will be raised at the last day. But unbelievers will be raised to death. Their bodies will be resuscitated and their senses restored—they will experience what happens to them. But what they experience will be the judgment of God, an existence apart from the love and goodness of God which the Bible calls "hell". This is how Jesus puts it: "A time is coming when all who are in their graves will hear his voice and come out—those who have done what is good will rise to live, and those who have done what is evil will rise to be condemned" (5 v 28-29). But the one who believes is promised resurrection to life.

Second, Jesus says why this is possible: "I am ... the life ... Whoever lives by believing in me will never die" (11 v 25-26). Praying to his Father later in John's Gospel, Jesus says, "Now this is eternal life: that they know you, the only true God, and Jesus Christ, whom you have sent" (17 v 3). So real life and real death are not just about physical existence, but about knowing or not knowing God.

This means people can be dead (in the sense of not knowing God) even while they are alive (in the sense of existing). In fact, this is true of everyone unless and until God breathes new life into us through the Spirit— spiritual life from the life-giving Spirit.

It means, too, that people can be alive even while they're dying. By believing in Jesus, we can have spiritual life even though our physical bodies are aging and decaying. And nothing can take that life away from us— not even physical death when it comes.

So anyone who believes is promised resurrection to life in the future (11 v 25) and resurrection life in the present (v 26)—life beyond death and life before death.

For the Jews, resurrection was thought to belong to a distant time beyond history. In Jesus, that time is already present because in Jesus resurrection has begun. Already we can know God and be energised by his Spirit. Resurrection now!

Death is the one thing none of us can avoid. We see and feel it at a distance in every stray grey hair and aching limb. Perhaps for you it looms closer still. But for those who believe in Jesus, death is not the end, because death leads on to resurrection. Death isn't the last word—resurrection is the last word. Christians might well fear dying—it can be a horrible, painful process. But Christians need not fear death, because for the Christian death leads to life—true life, eternal life.

Pray
Almighty God,
who through the death of your Son
has destroyed sin and death,
and by his resurrection
has restored innocence and everlasting life,
that we may be delivered
from the dominion of the devil,
and our mortal bodies raised up from the dead:
Grant that we may confidently
and wholeheartedly believe this,
and, finally, with your saints,
share in the joyful resurrection of the just;
through the same Jesus Christ, your Son, our Lord. Amen.

Martin Luther (1483-1546)

WEDNESDAY

John 11 v 25-27

Has anyone ever said to you, "I wish I had your faith"? What do they mean? "I can see your faith is comforting, but I'm not as gullible as you"? "I've tried believing, but I just don't feel anything"? I sometimes wish I could give them a treasure map with an X-marks-the-spot showing where a stash of faith can be found. "When you get there, help yourself."

The focus of these verses is not upon death or life, the present or the future. The focus is not even upon resurrection. Martha already knows about resurrection. She already believes in life after death. No, the focus of these verses is upon Jesus.

Jesus can promise resurrection to life in the future because *he himself* is the resurrection. And he can promise resurrection life in the present because *he himself* is the life. He is the promise and the prototype. His resurrection to life will become our resurrection.

Martha is a woman of faith, as we've seen. But having faith is not enough. Faith is not some special quality or attribute that qualifies you for heaven. What counts is Jesus. He's what qualifies us for heaven. Saving faith is simply the recognition of this. True faith involves trusting in Jesus. So what Jesus adds to Martha's faith is *himself*—the true and only object of saving faith. "Do you believes this?" he asks. He's not asking if she believes in the resurrection of the dead—she's already said she does. He's asking if she believes *he* is the resurrection. Christian faith is much more than believing certain things to be true. It's about entrusting yourself to a person: the Messiah, the Son of God (v 27).

Plenty of people believe in life after death in some sort of way. They believe their loved ones look down from above. Or they believe in reincarnation. Or they're just hoping for the best. But the Christian message is not simply that there is life after death, that death is not the last word, that there is hope. The Christian message is that there is life in Jesus, that Jesus is the last word, that there is hope in Jesus.

The crucial issue is not the size or strength of your faith. The crucial issue is the object of faith. Where's your trust? I might have tremendously strong faith that I can sail out to sea in a giant sieve, but it won't stop me from sinking. Or I might get on board a ferry, full of fear and anxiety, and cross safely across the English Channel to France.

So when someone says, "I wish I had your faith", what they ought to say is, "I wish I had your Saviour". But then the chances are they don't really want your Saviour, not as their Saviour and Lord.

You may feel you have very weak faith. You may wonder whether you really qualify as a Christian. That's irrelevant. The only question to ask is: *Do you believe Jesus* can save you? Do you believe there is life in him and only in him? The question is not: *Do you think your faith enough?* The question is: *Do you think Jesus is enough?* Let this be a comfort to you when your faith feels battered and shaky.

And notice that Martha's response of faith comes *before* Lazarus is raised from the dead. She still doesn't expect Jesus to raise him there and then (v 39). True faith is not just for the good times—when you see a miracle, when you have good health, when you have financial security. No, true faith is for the hard times—times of illness, stress, struggle and insecurity, when no miracle turns up. Ultimately, true faith must face the reality of death and still believe that Jesus is the resurrection and the life.

Meditate

My hope is built on nothing less
Than Jesus' blood and righteousness.
I dare not trust the sweetest frame,
But wholly trust in Jesus' Name.

His oath, his covenant, his blood,
Support me in the o'whelming flood.
When all around my soul gives way,
He then is all my hope and stay.

On Christ the solid Rock I stand,
All other ground is sinking sand.

Edward Mote (1797-1874)

THURSDAY

John 11 v 28-36

Mary comes to Jesus with the same words that Martha uses. Yet Jesus' response to her is very different. Luke's account of Jesus' visit to their home shows Martha as a matter-of-fact, down-to-earth hostess, concerned with what's right (Luke 10 v 38-42). So it's no surprise that here in John's Gospel Jesus engages her with matters of fact, with the right way of seeing the situation. Mary, in contrast, sat at Jesus' feet, listening to his words (Luke 10 v 39). She was so focused on the person that the practicalities of his visit passed her by. How does Jesus engage with her in her bereavement?

First, John tells us that "when Jesus saw her weeping ... he was deeply moved in spirit and troubled" (John 11 v 33). The Greek word translated "deeply moved" was more normally used for the snorting of horses. When used of people, it describes a cry of anger. Jesus sees the grief of Mary and responds with a visceral cry of anger.

This is not the way the world is meant to be. The beautiful world Jesus made with his Father is now scarred and broken. The world whose manufacture brought him such delight (Proverbs 8 v 30-31) is convulsed in grief.

The world which his Father once declared to be very good is now full of situations like this one, which are very bad.

None of this is new information to Jesus. After all, he has come into the world to cure this wound. But Mary's tears are a window onto a world of pain. They bring the brokenness of the world into the foreground. Jesus sees what sin and death have done in his world, and he is angry.

Then, Jesus bursts into tears (John 11 v 35). Not, I think, for Lazarus, since there is every indication he already knows how this story will end (v 11). This grief is the other side of his anger. He feels anger against the sin which has caused this grief. But he feels grief with those who suffer its effects. He was, says the 5th-century bishop Cyril of Alexandria, "not mourning Lazarus alone but all of humanity, which is subject to death, having justly fallen under so great a penalty." (Commentary on the Gospel of John 7)

The astonishing thing is that the one who weeps is the one whom John introduces as the Word of God, the Word who is God (1 v 1). The Word made flesh weeps with Mary. Jesus reveals a God who is not unfeeling or uncaring, but one who feels our infirmities and shares our grief—a God who is outraged by sin.

Sometimes in the middle of our hurt we cry out to God, "Why me? Why, Lord? Do you not care? Why are you letting this happen? My God, why have you forsaken me?" And we find that our cries are echoed by the Son of God, who cried on the cross, *"Eloi, Eloi, lema sabachthani?"*—which means, "My God, my God, why have you forsaken me?" (Mark 15 v 34). God himself identifies with the godforsaken. On the cross, he places himself with sinners and feels the full effects of sin. So cry out to Jesus, and know that he hears and grieves with you.

Let's end by reflecting on Jesus as the model of how we respond to those who grieve. Often we feel the need to talk and sometimes that's appropriate, as it was for Jesus with Martha. But sometimes it's enough simply to be with someone or to cry with them. "Jesus wept," says the 3rd-century theologian Hippolytus, "to give us an example of sympathy and kindliness toward our fellow human beings. Jesus wept that he might by deed rather than word teach us to 'weep with those that weep'" (Romans 12 v 15). And we need to open our hearts in prayer, and ask to see the world as God sees it, and to feel the grief that Jesus feels for a broken world. Sometimes it is enough to offer up our tears as prayers.

Meditate

The Spirit helps us in our weakness.
We do not know what we ought to pray for,
but the Spirit himself intercedes for us
through wordless groans.
And he who searches our hearts
knows the mind of the Spirit,
because the Spirit intercedes for God's people
in accordance with the will of God.

Romans 8 v 26-27

FRIDAY

John 11 v 36-44

"Words are cheap," we sometimes say. Someone can be gushing in their praise or fulsome in their expressions of intent. But it means nothing if their actions don't match their words.

Jesus has met Martha and comforted her. But are his words mere pious waffle? "I am the resurrection" is a great soundbite (#resurrectionhope). But how can she know it's true? After all, no one has come back from the dead to tell her what it's like.

Jesus has met Mary and wept with her. But is his reaction mere empty sentiment? His compassion may be a comfort, but it doesn't change anything. After all, when Jesus has finished crying and wiped away his tears, Mary is still bereaved.

But there is a third member of this family and Jesus is about to meet him too—Mary and Martha's deceased brother, Lazarus. And it's this third encounter that shows that Jesus' words are more than platitudes and his tears are more than sentiment. If the focus of Jesus' encounter with Martha was on faith, and with Mary it was on love, then with Lazarus the focus is upon hope. The story isn't complete without his resurrection.

From the beginning Jesus had told his disciples that Lazarus' illness would be "for God's glory" (v 4). He delayed his visit to create an opportunity to strengthen the faith of his disciples (v 6, v 15). Now, as he stands before the tomb, he prays aloud so others will overhear his prayer (v 41-42). This is a set piece, designed to prove that he is the resurrection and the life.

So it is that he calls Lazarus from the tomb by name (v 43). Back in 5 v 25 Jesus had said, "Very truly I tell you, a time is coming and has now come when the dead will hear the voice of the Son of God and those who hear will live". Now he makes good that claim. It's sometimes said Jesus had to call Lazarus by name, otherwise all the dead in their tombs would have come out with him!

And yet the raising of Lazarus is only a sign. It's not the real thing. Lazarus lived again, but not for ever. He's not still walking round Palestine, telling his story.

His resurrection pointed forward to Jesus' own resurrection. Jesus is life because he gives life; and Jesus gives life because he rose from the dead. And, whereas Lazarus came out struggling, his hands and feet bound with strips of cloth, Jesus left the grave clothes behind. He rose with a permanent, new resurrection body. Lazarus rose to die again. Jesus rose to live for ever.

The voice that called Lazarus from the grave is the voice we hear in the gospel message. "If he revived the body of Lazarus with his voice," says the German Reformer Caspar Cruciger, "he will certainly with the voice of the gospel kindle eternal life and righteousness in hearts according to his promise".

This is our great hope. We live in a sin-marred world. But sin will not be the last word; resurrection will be the last word. Sin and all its ugly offspring will be transformed in the new creation.

"If only you had been here…" say Martha and Mary (NLT). What is it that *you* would put after, "If only…"? What hope is there for your if-only in the promise of a new creation?

Meditate

I am the voice of life that wakens the dead.
I am the good odour that takes away the foul odour.
I am the voice of joy that takes away sorrow and grief.
I am the comfort of those who are in grief.
I am the joy of the whole world.
I gladden all my friends and rejoice with them.
I am the bread of life.

Athanasius (c. 296-373)

SATURDAY

John 11 v 45-53; 12 v 1-8

The story of Lazarus doesn't end with his resurrection. John shows us two responses to this miraculous event—a response of hate and a response of love.

First, the raising of Lazarus tips the religious leaders into action. But not, as you might expect, into welcoming Jesus as the Messiah. Quite the opposite. A man who can raise the dead is a dangerous prospect. "If we let him go on like this," they say, "everyone will believe in him, and then the Romans will come and take away both our temple and our nation" (11 v 48). They recognise that Jesus is offering credible proof of his claims. But rather than accepting those claims, their concern is the threat he poses to their own status. They hate their Roman overlords, but they opt to get rid of Jesus rather than disrupt the status quo. "So from that day on they plotted to take his life" (v 53).

Meanwhile in Bethany we see a very different response in chapter 12. Here is Martha doing what Martha does best—organising a meal. This is her act of love. And here is Mary, performing an outrageous, extravagant act of love. So extravagant it provokes the ire of Judas. Judas does the maths, works out the cost of the perfume splashed across the floor and raises his objection. He couches it as concern for the poor, but John says his real concern is himself (12 v 4-6).

Jesus comes to Mary's defence. "You will always have the poor among you," he says, "but you will not always have me" (v 8). He's alluding to Deuteronomy 15 v 10-11, where God commanded his people to show open-handed generosity to those in need "without a grudging heart"—the kind of grudging heart in Judas. The implication is that giving to the poor will normally be a good way of expressing our love for Jesus. But this is not a normal situation. Mary has a unique opportunity to lavish her love directly on Jesus.

Mingled into these two responses, John highlights two unwitting prophecies.

First, Caiaphas the high priest says, "It is better for you that one man die for the people than that the whole nation perish" (John 11 v 50). He has in mind only an act of political expediency. But John says Caiaphas spoke more than he realised. The cross was indeed an act in which one died for many—not to avert Roman retribution, but to avert divine retribution. John explains: "Jesus would die for the Jewish nation, and not only for that nation but also for the scattered children of God [that is, Gentile believers], to bring them together and make them one" (v 51-52).

Second, Jesus says Mary has anointed him "for the day of [his] burial" (12 v 7). Whether Mary saw it that way we can't know. But Jesus knew he would soon be killed. It's a strange end to the story. The story of Lazarus has proved that Jesus is the resurrection and the life. So why does he need to be prepared for burial? After all, he clearly has power over death. But Jesus came because death has power over you. He came for you. He came because it is better *for you* that one man die for his people than that the whole people of God perish. The resurrection died so that the dead could be raised.

So how are you going to respond? Will you grasp tightly your influence, your reputation, your comfort? Or will you willingly pour out your money, your time and your life in devotion to Jesus?

Pray

O sacred Head once wounded,
With grief and shame weighed down,
How scornfully surrounded
With thorns, thine only crown!
How pale art thou with anguish,
With sore abuse and scorn!
How does that visage languish
Which once was bright as morn!

Thy grief and bitter passion
Were all for sinners' gain.
Mine, mine was the transgression,
But thine the deadly pain.
Lo, here I fall, my Saviour;
'Tis I deserve thy place.
Look on me with thy favour,
Vouchsafe to me thy grace.

Paul Gerhardt (1607-1676),
trans. James W. Alexander (1804-1859)

THE FOURTH WEEK OF LENT

Seeing the Glory of the Cross

SUNDAY

John 12 v 20-50

What do you boast about? What makes you feel proud? What enhances your reputation?

Maybe it's your achievements. You've worked hard. You've done well. You've bought your home. You've got a pension. You're comfortable.

Maybe it's your education—your degree or your training. Or the knowledge you have or the books you've read.

Maybe it's your respectability. You can hold your head up high in the neighbourhood. People respect you. You're involved in local activities. You're an upstanding member of the community.

Maybe it's your religion. You go to church each Sunday. You say your prayers each day. You do the right thing.

What's your glory?

This passage is about the glory of Jesus. But his glory is not what we expect.

Pray

Pray through the reading by taking a verse or two at a time. Each time identify...
* *something to praise God for*
* *something to confess*
* *something to turn into a request*

MONDAY

John 12 v 20-26

There's an traditional English folk song which tells the story of John Barleycorn:

There were three men, came out of the west
Their fortunes for to try.
And these three men made a solemn vow:
John Barleycorn must die.
They ploughed, they sowed, they harrowed him in,
Threw clods upon his head
Till these three men were satisfied:
John Barleycorn was dead.

John Barleycorn, of course, is a corn of barley. In the verses that follow, he springs up from the grave only to be cut down with a scythe, beaten and mashed, and then he finally produces beer for the folk singer!

Jesus is using a similar image in these verses. He has just arrived in Jerusalem to great acclaim (v 12-16). His fame is spreading, especially the news that he can bring people back from the dead (v 17-18). So it's not surprising that a delegation of Greeks wants to see him (v 20-22). Jesus is about to go global, to become an international celebrity. "The whole world has gone after him!" (v 19).

At a number of points in John's Gospel, Jesus has said that his "hour has not yet come". But not anymore. Now he declares, "The hour has come for the Son of Man to be glorified" (v 23).

But there's a twist, because what King Jesus starts talking about next is not his throne or his court or his victories, but his death. This is his hour—the hour of his death. This is his glory—the glory of death.

But the cross of Jesus didn't look like glory! It looked like shame and defeat. It looked like suffering and failure. Crucifixion was brutal and bloody. You were stripped naked. Nails were driven through your wrists and feet. The weight of your body meant the only way you could breathe was to lift yourself up by pushing down on the nails through your feet, until finally, when you no longer had the strength to push your body up, you died of suffocation. Crucifixion was so terrible that Romans wouldn't mention it in polite company. It couldn't be done to a Roman citizen, no matter what crime they had committed. The Jews believed a crucified person was cursed by God (Deuteronomy 21 v 23).

How can this be the glory of Jesus? "Very truly I tell you," Jesus says, "unless a grain of wheat falls to the ground and dies, it remains only a single seed. But if it dies, it produces many seeds" (John 12 v 24). The glory of the cross is that through his death, Jesus will bring life to many.

This is where the image of a seed comes in. Think of an apple pip. On its own, it is just an inert, shrivelled-up stone. You bury it in the ground, in its soily grave. It's dead and buried. But then it bursts from the ground to produce a harvest of many apples.

In the same way, Jesus died. He was dead and buried. But he, too, burst from the ground. He, too, produced a great harvest—a harvest that continues to this very day.

Today, let your lunch be an unexpected reminder of Christ's unexpected glory! His death is his glory because it brings life. The death of one person brings life to many.

Meditate

We were therefore buried with him
through baptism into death in order that,
just as Christ was raised from the dead
through the glory of the Father,
we too may live a new life.

Romans 6 v 4

TUESDAY

John 12 v 27-33

No one likes doing hard things. None of us opt for pain. Unless, of course, we think it's going to be worth it. The marathon runner pushes through "the wall" because they look forward to the finishing line.

The student spends long hours in the library because they look forward to qualifying.

Jesus wouldn't opt for the cross. He's not a masochist. As he contemplates his death, he says, "Now my soul is troubled" (v 27). But he considers it worth it. He considers *you* worth it. "What shall I say?" he continues, "'Father, save me from this hour'? No, it was for this very reason I came to this hour" (v 27). In other words, *I could opt out, but this is why I came.* Jesus came to die to save many people.

And God the Father concurs. Jesus asks his Father to glorify him, and a voice from heaven confirms that he will glorify Jesus. This is the Father's affirmation not only of Jesus, but also of the cross. "One who does not seek the cross of Jesus," wrote St John of the Cross, "isn't seeking the glory of Christ".

Jesus talks about being "lifted up from the earth" (v 32). As we saw in John 3, this talk of "lifting up" is royal language. Jesus is about to ascend to the throne. He is going to be higher, lifted up, exalted. But John adds his own little editorial explanation: "He said this to show the kind of death he was going to die" (12 v 33). Jesus is going to be higher, lifted, exalted through his death. He will literally be lifted up onto the cross as spectators watch from below. But John is not just making some gruesome pun. Again, his point is that the death of Jesus is the glory of Jesus.

But what's the evidence that the cross equals glory— that it wasn't just the unfortunate end of a deluded individual 2000 years ago? "I, when I am lifted up from the earth, will draw all people to myself" (v 32). The cross equals glory because through the cross, Jesus will save all people—not just Jewish people, but Gentiles like the Greeks who've come to see him (v 20).

In other words, *we* are the proof! If you're a Christian, then *you* are the evidence that the cross equals glory. The first "evangelistic tract" was unwittingly hung by Pilate over the cross. It read: "Jesus of Nazareth, the King of the Jews". In three languages it proclaimed the kingship of Jesus to all the world (19 v 19-20).

It's a great encouragement to outreach. The death of Jesus will not be in vain. The Spirit of God draws all kinds of people to Jesus when they hear the message of his cross—when they hear the message of the cross *from you*. It's not always easy talking about Jesus with people. People do not want to hear. People may make us feel ashamed of our beliefs. But it's worth pushing through "the wall". For the death of Jesus will not be in vain—he *will* draw people to himself.

Meditate

I cannot tell how he will win the nations,
How he will claim his earthly heritage,
How satisfy the needs and aspirations
Of east and west, of sinner and of sage.
But this I know, all flesh shall see his glory,
And he shall reap the harvest he has sown,
And some glad day his sun will shine in splendour
When he the Saviour, Saviour of the world, is known.

William Young Fullerton (1857-1932)

WEDNESDAY

John 12 v 34-37

Back in the 1990s, Magic Eye pictures were popular. They appeared to be two-dimensional patterns. But if you squinted your eyes in just the right way, then you might have made out a three-dimensional image. In something of a wow-moment, a completely different image would leap into view.

The cross is like a Magic Eye picture. At first it just looks like a two-dimensional picture of a man dying in shame. But look with the eyes of faith, and a whole other dimension appears. The glory of God emerges from the scene.

This story starts with some Greeks asking to see Jesus. It's not clear whether their request is granted. Instead, as we've seen, Jesus says his glory is found in his death. His glory is a hidden glory. It's not what you expect and you might not recognise it.

This is exactly what we find in verse 34: "The crowd spoke up, 'We have heard from the Law that the Messiah will remain for ever, so how can you say, "The Son of Man must be lifted up"? Who is this "Son of Man"?'" The people are only seeing in two dimensions. They can't see how Jesus can be the Messiah if he's going to die. That's not what you expect from a glorious king!

Then, John says, Jesus "hid himself from them" (v 36). These Greeks can't see Jesus because he's hiding! It's a picture of the way Jesus hides himself from the proud. Proud people can't recognise Jesus— not the true Jesus.

We're given an example of this in verse 37: "Even after Jesus had performed so many signs in their presence, they still would not believe in him". People who have seen the power of Jesus firsthand still do not believe in him! John doesn't say they "*could* not believe", but they "*would* not". The Early Church Father Chrysostom comments, "Because they would not practice virtue therefore they cannot practice it" (Homilies on the Gospel of John 68.2). The religious leaders even plot to murder Lazarus to stop the news of Jesus spreading (v 9-11). Think about that for a moment. They plan to kill Lazarus because he came back from the dead! How's that going to work? They don't dispute his resurrection. But they refuse to accept its implications.

It's a picture of all humanity. As we saw in John 9, people reject Jesus because they are:

- *too proud to admit their need*
- *too proud to submit their lives*

So Jesus hides himself from the proud. Proud people can't recognise Jesus—not the true Jesus. And that's because the glory of Jesus is revealed in the cross—and that's a hidden glory.

It means that if you want to understand Jesus, the number one priority is not intellect, insight or piety. You don't start with academic interpretations or contemplative practices. The number one priority is humility. As you read the Bible, you need approach it with a willingness to admit your need for Jesus and submit your life to Jesus. And when we do that, we can have the privilege of becoming "children of light" (v 36).

Pray

O Lord Jesus Christ,
who didst humble thyself
to become man,
and to be born into the world
for our salvation:
teach us the grace of humility,
root out of our hearts
all pride and haughtiness,
and so fashion us
after thy holy likeness in this world,
that in the world to come
we may be made like unto thee
in thy eternal kingdom. Amen.

William Walsham How (1823-1897)

THURSDAY

John 12 v 37-43

" If you really want to know what makes me tick, then you need to realise that..." Has anyone said that to you? *You need to realise I'm obsessed with cycling. You need to realise I think coffee is evil. You need to realise I'm never happier then when I'm walking in the countryside.*

If you really want to know what makes Jesus tick, then you need to realise that he came to die. Look at Jesus without the cross and you'll misunderstand him.

But if you're proud, then you won't like the cross. Because the cross says you can't save yourself. Your goodness, your wisdom, your respectability are not enough. You're desperately needy. You're helpless and hopeless on your own. The cross humbles us.

John says this is exactly what the prophet Isaiah predicted: the proud would not recognise Jesus (v 38-41). In Isaiah 52 – 53 the prophet Isaiah talks about God's Servant being "lifted up and highly exalted". Then immediately Isaiah says, "There were many who were appalled at him—his appearance was so disfigured". Isaiah says God's Servant "was pierced for our transgressions, he was crushed for our iniquities". "We all, like sheep, have gone astray ... and the LORD has laid on him the iniquity of us all." But Isaiah also says this servant "will sprinkle many nations". He "will justify many".

Isaiah "saw Jesus' glory" (John 12 v 41). What did that glory look like? It looked like a man disfigured, crushed, punished. Isaiah saw the death of Jesus. But he also saw Jesus saving many people. He saw life through death and exaltation through shame—all the things Jesus has been saying in this conversation.

Isaiah also warns that the proud will not "get it". You will not see Christ unless you humble yourself to see his glory in his death. And by humility, I don't mean some kind of beautiful virtue you achieve. I mean being humiliated—recognising you have absolutely nothing to offer God. We like to think of ourselves as self-made people. But we need to be un-made before we can be re-made by God.

Some of the religious leaders believed in Jesus (v 42). Almost. They were so close to knowing God. But "they loved human praise more than praise from God" (v 43). They were too proud to know God.

We, too, often feel the pressure to make following Jesus respectable—to turn the Christian message into a call to be nice to others, or an ethical approach that our culture approves of. But the cross won't allow that. The cross doesn't fit in our culture. It's too bloody and brutal. It reveals our sin and our helplessness—and it humbles us. But listen to the words of Jesus:

Anyone who loves their life will lose it, while anyone who hates their life in this world will keep it for eternal

> *life. Whoever serves me must follow me; and where I*
> *am, my servant also will be. My Father will honour the*
> *one who serves me.* *(v 25-26)*

You can't follow Jesus if you want human praise. But anyone who embraces the cross will be honoured by God. Don't live today in fear of human rejection and in love with human approval—instead, seek the eternal honour that comes from being a humble servant of the Lord Jesus.

Meditate

> *By his passion he made atonement for our evil passions,*
> *by his death he cured our death,*
> *by his tomb he robbed the tomb,*
> *by the nails that pierced his flesh*
> *he destroyed the foundations of hell.*

> *Basil of Seleucia (5th century)*

FRIDAY

John 12 v 44-50

In the final round of the TV quiz show *Who Wants to Be a Millionaire?* the contestants must choose from four answers. Choose the right answer, and they walk away with a million pounds. Choose the wrong answer, and they don't.

Here Jesus poses a bigger question and more is at stake. What makes the difference is not how clever you are, but whether you'll admit your need and submit your life. This is not a test, but an invitation.

These verses are the conclusion not just of this encounter, but of the whole ministry of Jesus (the rest of John's Gospel is concerned with the events surrounding the death of Jesus). This is Jesus' final appeal.

People have told me they find Christianity "an interesting set of ideas", "an inspiring spirituality" or "a moral code I want to live by". But at stake is much more than whether you buy into a particular philosophy or spirituality or lifestyle. Jesus said, "Whoever believes in me does not believe in me only, but in the one who sent me" (v 44). At stake is whether you accept God or not. You're not accepting or rejecting a worldview. You're accepting or rejecting God.

Jesus adds, "The one who looks at me is seeing the one who sent me" (v 45). How do we look at Jesus? We look at the cross. So Jesus is saying, *If you see my glory in my death, then you see the glory of God himself.* "This is love: not that we loved God, but that he loved us and sent his Son as an atoning sacrifice for our sins" (1 John 4 v 10).

But there's more that is at stake. What we make of Jesus—and remember the real Jesus is the Jesus of the cross—will determine how we spend eternity (because Jesus speaks the words of God, John 12 v 49-50).

Jesus says, "There is a judge for the one who rejects me and does not accept my words; the very words I have spoken will condemn them at the last day" (v 48). This is a sobering statement. Our attitude to the cross rebounds on us. Jesus has already said, "Now is the time for judgment on this world" (v 31). No one listening thought the world was about to be judged. They all thought it was Jesus who was being judged. After all, he would be the one who ended up in the dock. But really *they* were the ones on trial.

And this is replicated every time someone hears the message of the cross. They make a judgment about what they hear. But that judgment rebounds on them. If we reject the cross, then we'll be rejected by God. If we accept the cross, then we'll be accepted by God. We seal our own fate.

Think of it as a life ring flung to a drowning man. What he makes of that life ring will determine his future. If he says, "I'm not taking hold of that—how embarrassing", then he'll drown. But if he clings onto it for all he's worth, then he'll be saved.

God sent his Son as a life ring to save you. If you say, "I'm not taking hold of that—how embarrassing", then you'll be condemned. But if you cling to the cross for all you're worth, then you will be saved. This is the "command [that] leads to eternal life" (v 50).

Where's your glory? Is it your achievements, your education, your respectability, your religion? The Bible invites us to boast in the cross. Why? Because in the cross we see the glory of Christ. Because in the cross we see the love of Christ. Christ left the glory of heaven. He humbled himself—even to death on the cross. He died like a grain of wheat to produce many seeds.

Pray

Nothing in my hand I bring,
Simply to the cross I cling;
Naked, come to thee for dress;
Helpless, look to thee for grace;
Foul, I to the fountain fly:
Wash me, Saviour, or I die.

Augustus Toplady, "Rock of Ages" (1740-1778)

SATURDAY

John 12 v 23-26

There's a twist in this story for those of us who would follow Jesus. As we've seen, Jesus talks about a seed falling to the ground and rising to produce a harvest. A seed in a packet does nothing. It just sits there, doing nothing, achieving nothing. But if you let it fall—if it dies (as it were) and you bury it in the ground—then it produces a harvest. Jesus is talking about his own death. Like a seed, he will die. But through his death, there'll be a harvest of life for many people.

But then Jesus says that anyone who serves him must follow him (v 26). "Anyone who loves their life will lose it, while anyone who hates their life in this world will keep it for eternal life" (v 25). The pattern for Jesus is the pattern for all his followers. If we give up our lives to him—if we die to self—then we'll produce a harvest.

How will we fulfil the task of mission—how will we bring a great harvest of people to know and follow Jesus? By dying to self—laying to rest our own preferences and priorities and pleasures—and through resurrection power.

Again and again in church history, setbacks have proved to be advances; failures have led to greater success. People have been martyred, and through their death many have come to know Christ. When I worked for Tearfund, one of our partners was involved with a church in Sudan whose building was bulldozed. The result? Four new churches sprang up across the neighbourhood. Others have died to self—giving up careers, wealth or comfort to advance the gospel—and through their sacrifice, life has come to many.

Often the persecutors of the church are like people blowing apart the head of a dandelion. All you're left with is a bare, empty stalk. Except that a hundred dandelion seeds have scattered, and up come new dandelions. That's not a good idea if you want a perfect lawn. But it's great news if you want to spread the fame of Jesus.

Paul says, "For we who are alive are always being given over to death for Jesus' sake, so that his life may also be revealed in our mortal body. So then, death is at work in us, but life is at work in you" (2 Corinthians 4 v 11-12). Behind every lively church and every missionary advance are people who are dying to self. Someone is arriving early to put out chairs, or staying up late to pray, or giving sacrificially, or accepting change they don't personally like.

In what way is God calling you to die to self today? Embrace it, knowing that in the mission of God, death leads to life.

Pray

O thou, who art the author of all good things
in thy holy Church,
work mightily in all thy servants,
that they may be profitable to all men,
and vessels of thy mercy and grace.
Control us all, and so govern our thoughts and deeds,
that we may serve thee in righteousness and true holiness;
and sanctify us all unto that eternal life,
which we, with all thy creatures,
groaning and travailing together, wait for and expect;
through Jesus Christ our Lord. Amen.

Philip Melanchthon (1497-1560)

THE FIFTH WEEK OF LENT

Seeing the Crucified King

SUNDAY

John 19 v 1-37

"What is truth?"

That's the question the Roman Governor Pilate asks in John 18 v 38. And it has never been more relevant. We live in a world of spin, PR and fake news. Spokesmen-and-women ought to be the truth-tellers in our society. But we routinely suspect them of distorting the truth. Our journalists are sometimes no better. It's hard to know what's news and what's propaganda.

Postmodernism has pointed out what Christians have always known: in this world what passes for truth is often the product of power. Those with power distort the truth to serve their own ends. We can't ask, "What is truth?" without also asking, "Who has power?"

All these issues are present at the trial of Jesus. Who is innocent and who is guilty? Who has power and who is powerless? And who can we trust?

Pray

Pray through the reading by taking a verse or two at a time. Each time identify…
- *something to praise God for*
- *something to confess*
- *something to turn into a request*

MONDAY

John 18 v 33 – 19 v 5

People sometimes ask me if I'm ordained. It's a simple enough question on the face it. But I never know how to answer. "No" is not really accurate, since I'm the pastor of a church. But "Yes" doesn't quite do the job either, because I suspect my view of what it means to be ordained is radically different from my questioner's. Their question comes with a set of assumptions that makes "Yes" as misleading as "No".

Something like this is going on in this encounter between Jesus and Pilate. Pilate asks Jesus, "Are you the king of the Jews?" (18 v 33). It's a simple enough question, and one that surely merits a yes or no answer. But Jesus can't give a yes or no answer without misleading Pilate. Yes, he is a king, but no, he's not a king in any sense that Pilate would recognise.

This is how Jesus himself puts it: "My kingdom is not of [or from] this world. If it were, my servants would fight to prevent my arrest by the Jewish leaders. But now my kingdom is from another place" (18 v 36). It's not that Jesus is the king of some ethereal realm unconnected to real life on earth. Jesus does lay claim to this earth. After all, he taught us to pray, "Your kingdom come … on earth" (Matthew 6 v 10). But his kingship operates in a totally different way.

Pilate is the representative of Caesar. And Caesar is king because he has a big army. He has the power to coerce. But the authority of Jesus is completely different. His servants don't fight for power.

The underlying problem is that in the Garden of Eden, Satan portrayed God's rule not as good but as tyrannical. Humanity believed this lie and therefore rejected God's rule—and we have continued to do this ever since. But we also rule in a way that reflects the lie. We get human authority wrong as well as getting God wrong. So human rule is self-serving and human rulers twist truth to serve their purposes. We think God's rule is like this, and so the coming of God's rule doesn't sound like good news. It's a vicious cycle.

But Jesus has come to witness to the truth about God's reign (John 18 v 37). Jesus is not a self-serving king. He's the Servant-King, who gives his life for his people.

This is what makes the mockery of the soldiers so poignant. They dress Jesus with a crown of thorns and a purple rob, and hail him as king. It's intended as a cruel and vicious satire. For Jesus appears to be completely in their power. Every slap across the face is meant to demonstrate that this king is no king at all.

But instead every slap proclaims that this king is the true King—the Servant-King, who gives his life for his people.

Is self-promotion a temptation you face? Do you long to be honoured or admired? Take an honest look: is that ever the motivation which underlies the way you interact with your children, or your junior colleagues, or people at church, or the waiter serving your food? The early church father Tertullian reminds us that Jesus wore a crown of thorns. This was the "honour" he received. So to those who long to be honoured, Tertullian says, "Go ahead, and be crowned as he was. You have my full permission." (The Chaplet 9.9)

When Pilate has Jesus wheeled out before the baying crowd, his words unwittingly sound a prophetic note: "Here is the man!" God created Adam—or "man", which is what "Adam" means—to rule over his world, to exercise the kingship of God. God created man on the sixth day. Now John describes the events of Good Friday—the sixth day of the week. *Let us make man*, God had said—a man to "rule". Now Pilate says, "Here is the man". Here is the man to rule in the way mankind has failed to, in the way *you* have failed to; here is the King to restore God's kingdom.

Pray

May the mind of Christ, my Saviour,
Live in me from day to day,
By His love and power controlling
All I do and say.

May the love of Jesus fill me
As the waters fill the sea;
Him exalting, self abasing,
This is victory.

Kate Wilkinson (1859-1928)

TUESDAY

John 19 v 5-11

Who's in charge as Jesus stands trial?

Pilate is the obvious choice. He has the backing of the Roman Empire with a cohort of soldiers on hand in case anyone doubts it. As he reminds Jesus, "I have power either to free you or to crucify you" (v 10). And yet, despite the fact he can "find no basis for a charge against him" (v 6), Pilate cannot acquit Jesus because he fears the mob.

At the same time, the thought of condemning Jesus fills him with fear, especially when he learns that Jesus claims to be the son of a god. So he "tried to set Jesus free" (v 12). He tried, but he failed. Whatever formal power Pilate has, he is quite clearly not in control.

Instead it's the Jewish leaders who seem to be running the show, manipulating Pilate at every turn. But they have no legal authority to carry out the execution, as they remind Pilate in 18 v 31.

In the middle of the chaos and confusion stands Jesus. And he is silent (19 v 9).

Pilate believes the might of Roman power is the ultimate authority. But Jesus reminds him that there is a higher power (v 11). Military power, political power and

social power are not the last word. All power is accountable to God.

To a greater or lesser extent, we all exercise authority—in the home, in the workplace, in the community or
in the church. That power is given to us "from above".
And we are accountable for its use. How might that
affect your use of authority today?

Jesus is being judged by Pilate. The Jewish leaders have
already formed their verdict. And so they cry, "Crucify!
Crucify!"

"The one who handed [Jesus] over to [Pilate]" in verse
11 is probably the Jewish leaders, and the high priest
Caiaphas in particular (compare with 18 v 30, 35).
Caiaphas is intent on securing Jesus' death, while Pilate
is only a reluctant participant, too spineless to resist
their manipulation. In the sovereign plan of God, he
finds himself in a situation he didn't look for (v 11). So
the sin of Caiaphas is greater. But Pilate is still culpable
for his judgment on Jesus.

And so are we. Each day people judge Jesus. Every
one of us forms a verdict on his claims. People reject
his kingship over their lives. In today's court of public
opinion, the majority verdict is that Jesus is no King
worth following. And as we look around us, it seems
that they're getting away with it.

But the sobering reality is that, ultimately, this judgment will rebound on us. By rejecting Jesus as our King,

we demonstrate that we are rebels against God. Pilate thinks his is the last word on justice. He will decide whether Jesus lives or dies. But there is a higher court than Pilate's, a higher court than public opinion—a heavenly court of appeal. The case will be reviewed, and through the resurrection, the verdict will be overturned.

Meditate

The head that once was crowned with thorns
Is crowned with glory now;
A royal diadem adorns
The mighty Victor's brow.

The cross he bore is life and health,
Though shame and death to him;
His people's hope, his people's wealth,
Their everlasting theme.

Thomas Kelly (1769-1855)

WEDNESDAY

John 19 v 12-22

In 2006, England played in the finals of the World Cup. Scotland had failed to qualify. So who did the Scots support? According to T-shirts being sold in Glasgow, it was "ABE"—Anyone But England. It's an example of the good-natured banter beloved of sports fans the world over (though some people chose to take offence).

Humanity's allegiance is much more significant. This is a life-and-death issue. And who does humanity support? "ABJ". Anyone But Jesus.

It's worth standing back to recognise what takes place in these verses. John labours the point. Three times Pilate says, "I find no basis for a charge against him" (18 v 38; 19 v 4, 6). There's no doubt about it: Pilate thinks Jesus is innocent. Yet for the sake of political expediency, "Pilate handed him over to [the chief priests] to be crucified" (v 16). He condemns a man he knows to be innocent. That sounds outrageous—but I wonder, are there times when *you* find it expedient to ignore the claims of Jesus?

Actually, it gets worse. Not only does Pilate condemn an innocent man; he also pardons a guilty man. The custom was for the Romans to release a Jewish prisoner to mark the Passover Festival. Pilate offers them a choice between Jesus—an obviously innocent man—and Barabbas—an obviously guilty man. They choose Barabbas (18 v 39-40). Anyone But Jesus.

For John, this is another picture of the meaning of the cross. The innocent dies that the guilty may go free. *We are all Barabbas.* "Barabbas," John tells us, "had taken part in an uprising" (18 v 40). And we are part of humanity's uprising against God. Yet it's Jesus who bears our guilt so we can walk free.

What about the religious leaders? At first glance, their words might surprise us. After all, the Jews hated Caesar. He represented the empire which had subjugated their nation and occupied their land. And not just their land—this was *God's* land. It was an act of sacrilege.

But, when Pilate says, "Here is your king" (v 14), all of a sudden they care deeply about Caesar's honour. "We have no king but Caesar," they cry (v 15). They not only reject Jesus; they reject all messianic claims. When Pilate orders an ironic notice of the kingship of Jesus to be placed over his cross, the religious leaders protest (v 19-22). Anyone But Jesus.

The chances are you've told someone about Jesus and been rebuffed or mocked. It's easy to take it personally. It's tempting to wonder if you did something wrong. But humanity has a deep-seated bias against God. The trial of Jesus is humanity's verdict writ large. When we get the chance, we murder our Creator. And so still today people support "ABJ". As Christians, our response must be to persevere and pray—the story is not over yet.

Meditate

Look, ye saints, the sight is glorious.
See the Man of Sorrows now,
From the fight returned victorious.
Every knee to him shall bow:
Crown him! Crown him!
Crowns become the Victor's brow.

Sinners in derision crowned him,
Mocking thus the Saviour's claim;
Saints and angels crowd around him,
Own his title, praise his name:
Crown him! Crown him!
Spread abroad the Victor's fame!

Thomas Kelly (1769-1855)

THURSDAY

John 19 v 23-29

With hushed tones, we stand before the cross. For the soldiers gambling for Jesus' garments it was just another day, another crucifixion. But John points us beyond the events to see their meaning. Twice in this account he talks about the fulfilment of Scripture (v 24, 28).

The night before, Jesus had humbly removed his outer clothing to wash the disciples' feet (13 v 4). Now that love goes further as he's stripped of his undergarment as well. But his one-piece undergarment can't be split between the soldiers, so they cast lots for it. It's such a small incident, given everything else that's taking place. But it fulfils what David had said in Psalm 22 v 18. David was Israel's greatest king—the archetypal king. But Psalm 22 is a reminder that he was also a suffering king. So the sufferings of Jesus don't invalidate his claim to be the Messiah, God's promised King. Quite the opposite. The fact that he suffers like David *proves* his claim.

John makes a similar point with his second reference to the fulfilment of Scripture. Jesus says, "I am thirsty", echoing another psalm in which David said, "They … gave me vinegar for my thirst" (Psalm 69 v 21).

But there is more going on with this declaration of thirst. Throughout John's Gospel, Jesus has been the Thirst-Quencher.

> *Everyone who drinks this water will be thirsty again, but whoever drinks the water I give them will never thirst. Indeed, the water I give them will become in them a spring of water welling up to eternal life. (4 v 13-14)*
>
> *Whoever believes in me will never be thirsty. (6 v 35)*
>
> *Let anyone who is thirsty come to me and drink. Whoever believes in me, as Scripture has said, rivers of living water will flow from within them. (7 v 37-38)*

But to be the Thirst-Quencher, Jesus must thirst. He experiences the emptiness we deserve that we might be filled. He is cut off from God that we might be satisfied in God.

We also need to go back to the first miracle that Jesus performed at the wedding of Cana (2 v 1-12). Then, in a moment of need, Jesus turned water into wine. And not just any old wine, but *the best of wine*. It was a powerful symbol of the new life he was bringing that would sweep away the old, broken religious systems. But now, at his moment of need, Jesus himself is offered wine vinegar, *the worst of wine*. Jesus gets the worst to give us the best. Sometimes we're tempted to feel short-changed by life. But when we look at the cross, we see it isn't so—Jesus died to quench our thirst with the very best.

Yet John highlights the fulfilment of Scripture not simply to point us to the meaning of the cross. He also wants to demonstrate that this was all thought out in advance. What's happening is not happening by chance. Events for Jesus have not spun out of his control. It's all part of a plan, an eternal plan, agreed between the Father and the Son, promised in the Old Testament. Though Jesus is dying, he's still in control. As he said in 10 v 18, "No one takes [my life] from me, but I lay it down of my own accord. I have authority to lay it down and authority to take it up again. This command I received from my Father." This is all part of the plan— the plan to save you.

Meditate

Condemned to death though innocent,
he went forward bearing on his shoulders
the cross on which he was to suffer.
He did this for our sake, taking on himself the
punishment that the law justly imposed on sinners ...
We who have all committed many sins were under that
ancient curse for our refusal to obey the law of God.
To set us free he who was without sin took that curse on himself.
Since he is God who is above all,
his sufferings sufficed for all,
his death in the flesh was the redemption of all.
And so, Christ carried the cross,
a cross that was rightfully not his but ours.

Cyril of Alexandria (c. 376 – 444)

FRIDAY

John 19 v 30

The last words of the playwright George Bernard Shaw, spoken to his nurse, were, "Sister, you're trying to keep me alive as an old curiosity, but I'm done, I'm finished, I'm going to die". Shaw's life was over and nothing could be done for him.

At first sight the last words of Jesus in John's account are similar: "It is finished". But the meaning of these words was very different.

The passion of Jesus is finished. This is the end of the earthly life of Jesus. But this is not a cry of defeat. From the beginning—when the guards arresting Jesus fell before him (18 v 6)—to this final moment, everything points to the triumph of Jesus. Jesus is in control: he lays down his life of his own accord (10 v 18). And throughout his Gospel, John has spoken of Jesus as exalted on the cross. This is a cry of triumph.

So too *the work of the Father is finished.* The previous night, as he looked ahead to the events of the first Good Friday, Jesus had prayed, "I have brought you glory on earth by finishing the work you gave me to do" (17 v 4). The Father gave Jesus a job to do—to reveal God to the world and to reconcile the world to God. And now that job has been completed: on the cross Jesus is revealing the full extent of God's love and he is reconciling humanity to God by covering our sin.

The plan of salvation is finished. Moments before Jesus uttered his final words, we read, "Knowing that everything had now been finished, and so that Scripture would be fulfilled, Jesus said, 'I am thirsty'" (19 v 28). The same word, "finished", is used both by John in verse 28 and by Jesus in verse 30. "It is finished" because Scripture is fulfilled. The plan of salvation, conceived in eternity and promised in Scripture, has reached its climax.

Think what this means for a moment. "It is finished" doesn't simply point to the meaning of the cross. It points to the meaning of history. In eternity past, Father and Son conceived a plan which had this moment as its centrepiece. The universe—every star and galaxy—was created to set the stage for this moment in the drama of God's love.

And wonderfully, *the striving of God's people is finished.* "It is finished" are words we need to keep on hearing. We need to say them to ourselves; we need to say them to one another. That's because we so easily default back to thinking we need to make ourselves good enough for God. We think we need to prove ourselves.

- *Some of us are over-busy because we find identity in our work.*
- *Some of us fill our lives with restless activity because we desperately seek fulfilment.*
- *Some of us self-harm to atone for the guilt that nags at our souls.*
- *Some of us find that no matter how much we do, it never seems enough.*

And all the time Jesus says, "It is finished". Everything that is needed has been done.

In those days, "It is finished" was written on a bill when it had been paid—it was the first-century equivalent of "Paid in full". Jesus has written over your life, "Paid in full". As the Chinese church leader Watchman Nee said, "Christianity begins not with a big do, but with a big done". So stop striving—it is finished.

Meditate

Hark! the voice of love and mercy
Sounds aloud from Calvary.
See, it rends the rocks asunder,
Shakes the earth, and veils the sky:
"It is finished!"
Hear the dying Saviour cry;

"It is finished!" O what pleasure
Do these precious words afford.
Heav'nly blessings without measure
Flow to us from Christ the Lord:
"It is finished!"
Saints, the dying words record.

Finished all the types and shadows
Of the ceremonial law.
Finished all that God had promised;
Death and hell no more shall awe:
"It is finished!"
Saints, from hence your comfort draw.

Jonathan Evans (1748-1809)

SATURDAY

John 19 v 31-37

Victims of crucifixion suffocated to death. They were suspended on the nails through their wrists so their arms constricted their lungs. They had to push up on their legs to breathe. They died when they no longer had the strength to do this. It could take days. Breaking their legs hastened this eventual end.

The Jews don't want the crucified bodies—cursed as they were by God, according to Deuteronomy 21 v 22-23—hanging there outside Jerusalem on the Sabbath, especially the Sabbath in the Passover week. So they ask Pilate to have the victims' legs broken and their bodies removed. But the soldiers find Jesus already dead. To make sure, one of them pierces his side. After death, the bodily fluids separate. So the flow of clear liquid along with blood was a sign that Jesus was really dead.

Jesus' resurrection was so unlikely and so unexpected that people since have claimed that he merely fainted and then revived in the cool of the tomb. But John was there. He saw the water. "The man who saw it has given testimony, and his testimony is true. He knows that he tells the truth, and he testifies so that you also may believe..." So that you, the reader, may believe that Jesus really died and really rose again (John 19 v 35).

But there's another reason why this detail matters to John. It means that none of Jesus' bones were broken. And this, says John, "happened so that the scripture would be fulfilled: 'Not one of his bones will be broken'" (v 36).

This doesn't come from a word of prediction in the conventional sense. It's not that a prophet said, "One day this will happen", and now it's happened. These words come from the Passover rule book. They describe how the Israelites were to treat the lamb: "They must not leave any of it till morning or break any of its bones. When they celebrate the Passover, they must follow all the regulations" (Numbers 9 v 12).

John's message is clear: Jesus is the ultimate Passover lamb. John has already reminded us that the crucifixion is taking place in the middle of the Passover Festival (John 19 v 31). Jesus is the one who sets us free from sin and dies in our place—just as the Passover lamb died in the place of the Israelites and led to their liberation from Egypt.

> *For you know that it was not with perishable things*
> *such as silver or gold that you were redeemed from*
> *the empty way of life handed down to you from your*
> *ancestors, but with the precious blood of Christ, a*
> *lamb without blemish or defect. He was chosen before*
> *the creation of the world, but was revealed in these last*
> *times for your sake.*   *(1 Peter 1 v 18-20)*

This is God's salvation plan, carefully woven from the beginning of time. And it was all "for your sake", says Peter. So today, take a moment to look on the one *you* have pierced (John 19 v 37). Behold the glory of the cross—and worship the Lamb, who loved you.

Pray

Rock of Ages, cleft for me,
Let me hide myself in thee;
Let the water and the blood,
From thy riven side which flowed,
Be of sin the double cure,
Cleanse me from its guilt and power.

Augustus Toplady (1740-1878)

HOLY WEEK & EASTER SUNDAY

The Triumph of the Cross

PALM SUNDAY

John 20 v 1-31

Palm Sunday is the day when we remember the triumphal entry of Jesus into Jerusalem (12 v 12-15). As he entered the city, the crowds acclaimed him as their king: "Hosanna! Blessed is he who comes in the name of the Lord! Blessed is the king of Israel!" (v 13)

What a difference a week makes. Just five days later the crowd was crying, "Crucify him!" (19 v 15). Jesus was a massive disappointment. While he was performing his miracles, it all looked so promising—here was someone with the power to overthrow the Roman occupiers. But now those in power have had the last word, as they always do. They have executed Jesus. And what use is a dead king?

But the story isn't over. And the last word has not yet been spoken. The defeat of Jesus is not what it seems. He is about to step from the grave, clear his throat and end his silence.

Pray

Pray through the reading by taking a verse or two at a time. Each time identify...
• something to praise God for
• something to confess
• something to turn into a request

MONDAY

John 20 v 1-10

Let's start with a quiz. What are the following phobias? Claustrophobia? Arachnophobia? Haemophobia? Dentophobia? Ablutophobia? Acrophobia?

The answers, in case you didn't know, are the fear of confined spaces, spiders, blood, dentists, washing and heights. There are many, many other named phobias. We live in a world of fear. I wonder what makes you afraid. What makes you panic?

It's panic we meet at the beginning of John's account of the resurrection. There's a lot of running about. Mary is running in panic in verse 2, and then Peter and John run in verse 4. As would you, if you thought someone was desecrating the remains of a loved one. Imagine you went to visit the grave of a recently deceased relative and found it had been dug up. You might well run for help as Mary did, or run to the grave as Peter and John did. Grave-robbing was a big issue at the time. A few years later the Emperor Claudius had to make it a capital offence in an attempt to stamp it out.

So they run, expecting the grave to have been desecrated. And what do they find? Order. The emphasis on running is replaced by an emphasis on the grave clothes. Verse 5 says John "looked in at the strips of linen lying there". We get almost the same phrase in verse 6, except it's Peter's turn to see "the strips of linen lying there". Then verse 7 describes the head cloth in great detail. John is telling a big story in a few words and yet he makes time to give us this detail on linen!

If you're burgling a house, you don't tidy up after yourself! You're in a hurry. You grab and run. And if you were robbing a grave or moving a body, then you would keep the grave clothes on. It would make life easier and less smelly. And we're talking about yards of cloth, wrapped round the body with spices between the layers. And that's the point: these grave clothes are not even ripped off. The language used suggests they were folded in an orderly fashion.

Imagine the scene from Peter's perspective. Mary runs from the tomb in a panic. It takes a while to catch what she's saying. But eventually you work out that the body of Jesus is missing. And then you too panic. Then you too run. A thousand thoughts flood your mind. Is it robbers? Is it too late? Could you confront them? Or is it the religious leaders? Could you get the Romans involved? What if they're already involved—what if they sanctioned this? Ahead of you, John looks in but does nothing. Is someone inside? Are they armed? Or is he repulsed by desecration? And so you arrive—flustered, sweaty, breathless. You burst in, ready for action… and what do you find? A neat stack of laundry. No violence, no chaos, no confusion. Just a pile of linen.

The disciples run to the rescue and find everything under control. In fact in verse 10 they just go back home. There's nothing for them to do! Everything is under control.

What makes you rush around in panic? Think about what it is that fills you with fear. And then in your head, play out your worst-case scenario. What does it look like? Ultimately, all our worst fears end in death. Health and safety, our despair about ageing, our fear of losing relationships—these are all reflections of our underlying fear of death. But if there is life beyond death, then we have no reason to be afraid. There is no need to panic. Everything is under control.

Meditate

Jesus lives! Thy terrors now
Can, O Death, no more appal us.
Jesus lives! By this we know
Thou, O Grave, canst not enthral us. Hallelujah!

Jesus lives! Henceforth is death
But the gate of Life immortal.
This shall calm our trembling breath,
When we pass its gloomy portal. Hallelujah!

Jesus lives! To him the throne
Over all the world is given.
We, in spirit with him one,
Rest and reign with him in heaven. Hallelujah!

Christian Fürchtegott Gellert (1715-1769),
trans. Frances Elizabeth Cox (1812-1897)

TUESDAY

John 20 v 11-18

I'm sure you've seen television shows in which we, the audience, know a long-lost relative is off-stage. But the person concerned has no idea they're about to be reunited with their loved one. As this passage opens, that's what is about to happen to Mary. We can see it coming, but she has no idea.

Mary's panic has given way to grief. We're told in verse 11 that Mary is crying, and then that she's weeping.

Indeed, Mary is so grief-stricken that it seems she doesn't even notice two angels! They ask, "Woman, why are you crying?" (v 13). And she doesn't say, "Wow, you're angels!" In fact, this is one of the few occasions in the Bible where someone doesn't fall down in fear when they see an angel. She barely seems to notice because she's so fixated on the missing body of Jesus.

Then it happens all over again, but this time with Jesus himself. He asks the exact same question: "Woman, why are you crying?" (v 15). Again, she expresses her distress, oblivious to who is standing in front of her.

And then he says, "Mary" (v 16). Now she recognises him—and grabs hold of him. It's as if she is saying to herself, *This time I am never going to let go. I'm not going to let that happen again. I'm never letting him out of my grip.* So

Jesus says in verse 17, "Do not hold on to me, for I have not yet ascended to the Father. Go instead to my brothers and tell them, 'I am ascending to my Father and your Father, to my God and your God.'"

The resurrection means so many things. It is the confirmation of a finished sacrifice. It is the sign of our reconciliation to God. It is the promise of a new creation. But for Mary, the resurrection is personal. And so it is with us too. Our Saviour lives. He is present with us by his Spirit, and one day we will see him face to face—he'll be as real to us then as he was to Mary that morning.

But Mary's relationship with Jesus is not just for her. This encounter can't just be about Mary and Jesus. Jesus has a job for her to do. This is news to be shared. It's the same for us. If you pursue a cosy spiritual experience with Jesus on your own, he'll prove to be very elusive. You find Jesus in serving him. You discover more of him as you tells others about him, until that day when you will stand before him.

Meditate

I know that my Redeemer lives—
What comfort this sweet sentence gives!
He lives, he lives, who once was dead,
And reigns, my ever-living Head!

He lives to silence all my fears,
To wipe away my falling tears,
To soothe and calm my troubled heart,
All needed blessings to impart.

Samuel Medley (1738-1799)

WEDNESDAY

John 20 v 17

Wouldn't it be great if Jesus were on earth today? Imagine if he had stayed on, never growing old. Imagine he was still preaching, still performing miracles. Surely that would make it easier to believe. Surely mission events would be easier if you could invite Jesus himself as your guest speaker.

Perhaps. But then again, perhaps not.

Mary must let go of Jesus because he still has work to do. His sufferings may be finished (19 v 30), but Jesus must still ascend to heaven so that his Father might become our Father. When you believe in Christ, you become united to Christ. He calls us brothers (20 v 17). And because we're united to Jesus and because he is with his Father, then we too are in the presence of the Father. His Father becomes our Father. According to the 5th-century theologian Cyril of Jerusalem, Jesus describes God as "my Father" because he is a Son by nature, and as "our Father" because every believer is now a son-and-heir by adoption. What is Christ's by nature becomes ours by grace.

Mary clings to Jesus. She wants him close for ever. But Jesus leaves his friends on earth in order to create a relationship that is more intimate, more secure and more precious.

- *Our relationship with Jesus now is more intimate, because Jesus dwells in us by his Spirit. Even though Jesus has left us in body, he now lives within us by the Spirit (14 v 16-18). And that doesn't mean we've received an inferior substitute. For the Son and the Spirit are of one being. The Spirit is the Spirit of Christ. We've received Jesus through the Spirit.*
- *Our relationship with Jesus now is more secure, because Jesus is our advocate before the Father (1 John 2 v 1-2). Because we're united with Christ, we can only be banished from God's presence if Jesus is banished from God's presence!*
- *Our relationship with Jesus now is more precious, because Jesus shares his sonship with us. Once Jesus had to ask the Father on our behalf. Now we can go to God as our Father directly through our link with Jesus (John 16 v 23-24).*

"Who is it you are looking for?" asks Jesus in 20 v 15. I think John poses that question to us as we read. When you feel disappointed by politicians, who are you looking for? When you invest your hopes in sports teams or film stars, who are you looking for? When you read romantic novels, who are you looking for? When you look at porn, who are you looking for? When you dream of Mr or Miss Right, who are you looking for?

Jesus offers us a relationship with himself that is more intimate, more secure and more precious than holding him with your hands. There is no need to look anywhere else.

Pray

We love thee, O our God,
and we desire to love thee more and more.
Grant to us that we may love thee
as much as we desire, and as much as we ought.
O dearest Friend, who hast so loved and saved us,
the thought of whom is so sweet
and always growing sweeter,
come with Christ and dwell in our hearts;
then thou wilt keep a watch
over our lips, our steps, our deeds,
and we shall not need to be anxious
either for our souls or our bodies.
Give us love, sweetest of all gifts,
which knows no enemy.
Give us in our hearts pure love,
born of thy love to us,
that we may love others as thou lovest us.
O most loving Father of Jesus Christ,
from whom floweth all love,
let our hearts, frozen in sin,
cold to thee and cold to others,
be warmed by this divine fire.
So help and bless us in thy Son. Amen.

Anselm (c. 1033-1109)

THURSDAY

John 20 v 19-28

We sometimes assume ancient people were gullible. They believed in the resurrection, we suppose, because they would believe in anything.

But it's not true. It's a kind of chronological snobbery—this assumption that we're smarter than ancient people. But Thomas demands evidence. He's not a gullible fool. He needs proof. He wants to be able to touch Jesus. He's a sceptic.

No one expected the resurrection. It wasn't that resurrection was an idea in the culture that people could readily jump to. The Greeks and Romans didn't believe people could come back to life. When Paul spoke in Athens, his Greek audience were with him until he mentioned the resurrection of the dead. Then, we're told, "some of them sneered" (Acts 17 v 32). In Greek culture, the idea of someone rising from the dead was laughable. Jewish opinion was divided. The Sadducees rejected the idea of resurrection altogether. Other Jews did believe in the resurrection, but only at the end of time. What no one expected was someone rising from the dead in the middle of history.

Without exception, when the risen Jesus appeared to people, they were shocked and surprised. They mistook him for someone else (as Mary did) or thought he was a ghost. They didn't see it coming—even though Jesus had told them it would happen!

Or perhaps you think the resurrection was an elaborate hoax. The problem is that it's not clear who would organise such a hoax. The opponents of Jesus didn't *want* him to rise again. And the followers of Jesus didn't *expect* him to rise again.

The best explanation for the resurrection is the one given by those who were there. And something happens which overcomes Thomas' scepticism—he is confronted with the risen Jesus. Thomas is not having a moment of enlightenment. He's not hallucinating or just remembering Jesus. He's not embracing some enduring ideals. Sometimes people have tried to reinterpret the resurrection in these kinds of terms. But Thomas is confronted with the physical reality of a once-dead man. *Hear, see, touch.* "Put your finger here … put it into my side" (John 20 v 27). It's not just *touch*. It's *get inside*. Get inside the flesh of a resurrected body.

Thomas' doubts are met with the reality of resurrection as he encounters the physical body of Jesus. And so he cries, "My Lord and my God!" (v 28). John's Gospel begins, "In the beginning was the Word, and the Word was with God, and the Word was God … The Word became flesh" (1 v 1, 14). Now, at the end of the story, Thomas meets the Word in resurrected flesh and proclaims that the Word is God.

Back in the sixth century, Gregory the Great said, "It was not an accident that that particular disciple was not present [when Jesus first appeared to his disciples in 20 v 19-23]. The divine mercy ordained that a doubting disciple should, by feeling in his Master the wounds of the flesh, heal in us the wounds of unbelief" (Forty Gospel Homilies 26). Perhaps you sometimes doubt the resurrection. You wish you didn't, but it just seems so impossible. God wrote this story into history *for you*. So let it reassure you. At Easter, scepticism meets reality—physical reality—so that doubt can give way to faith.

Pray

Lord, I do believe;
help me overcome my unbelief.
Lord, I love you;
may my love be undivided.
Lord, I hope for you;
set my heart on things above.
Amen.

GOOD FRIDAY

John 20 v 6-7, 23

I magine you heard a personal message from God: *Your sins are forgiven.* Is there something that plagues you with guilt? Is there a sin you keep committing? Do you hide a terrible secret? Imagine God saying, *Your sins are forgiven.*

The Easter story is just such a message of forgiveness and liberation. But we need the events of *both* Good Friday *and* Easter Sunday in order to hear it.

There are similarities between the resurrection of Jesus and the story of Lazarus in John 11. But the differences are more important. While both stories emphasise the grave clothes, Lazarus was still parcelled up in his. Presumably he had to shuffle out of the tomb. He had be released from the linen (11 v 44). In contrast, Jesus leaves his burial clothes behind. The implication is not that the strips of linen are lying in a corpse shape as if the body of Jesus has dissolved. The language suggests that they have been stacked because they're no longer needed.

Lazarus emerged *back* into our world. But Jesus steps *forward* into God's new world. And, as he steps out of the tomb, he leaves death behind. He has no need for grave clothes. He will never need them again. He is the firstfruits of a new creation, bursting with new life. For Lazarus, death was merely postponed. But Jesus has left it behind, neatly folded in a corner of a tomb.

The message of Easter is not simply that someone has risen from the dead. That had happened before. The message of Easter is that the Crucified One has risen. The One who died bearing the punishment for our sin has risen. The events of Good Friday are a senseless tragedy without Easter Sunday. And without Good Friday, Easter Sunday only offers hope for perfect people like Jesus. And that means *only* Jesus.

But the Crucified One has risen. The resurrection is the triumph of the cross.

This is why Easter Sunday comes with a mandate to bring forgiveness (20 v 23). Jesus is talking about the preaching of the gospel. If people reject the Easter message, then they're not forgiven, because Jesus is the only way to the Father (14 v 6). But if people respond to the Easter message with faith, then the message on earth is confirmed by the verdict of heaven.

Your sins are forgiven. You may hear those words from the mouth of a preacher or in the counsel of a friend. But it is a message from God for those with the faith to hear it: *Your sins are forgiven.*

Easter Sunday comes with the offer of forgiveness because the resurrection is God's great "Yes" to the cross. "It is finished," cried Jesus on Good Friday. *Yes, it is,* responds his Father on Easter Sunday. Sin has been atoned for and death has been defeated.

Your sins are forgiven.

Meditate

The strife is o'er, the battle done;
The victory of life is won;
The song of triumph has begun: Alleluia!

The powers of death have done their worst;
But Christ their legions hath dispersed;
Let shouts of holy joy outburst: Alleluia!

He broke the bonds of death and hell;
The bars from heaven's high portals fell;
Let hymns of praise his triumphs tell! Alleluia!

Lord, by the stripes which wounded thee,
From death's dread sting thy servants free,
That we may live, and sing to thee: Alleluia!

12th-century Latin hymn,
trans. France Pott (1832-1909)

SATURDAY

John 20 v 29-31

Mary and Thomas got to touch the risen Christ. The other disciples saw and heard him. But what about us? We can't inspect the empty tomb or see the folded grave clothes. We can't touch the resurrected body of Jesus.

Each story in John's resurrection account ends with a hint that this story is for us. The events at the tomb end with John describing his own reaction in the third person: "He saw and believed. (They still did not understand from Scripture that Jesus had to rise from the dead.)" (v 8-9).

Jesus had spoken of his resurrection back at the beginning of his ministry. John tells us that "after he was raised from the dead, his disciples recalled what he had said. Then they believed the Scripture and the words that Jesus had spoken" (2 v 22). How did the disciples believe in the resurrection? Through the Scriptures and the words of Jesus. John then describes people who believed in Jesus because they saw his miracles. But, says John, "Jesus would not entrust himself to them, for he knew all people" (2 v 24). They didn't have *true* faith. They were fair-weather followers—more interested in the miracles than in Jesus himself.

Now at the tomb, John seems to put himself in the same category. He sees and believes. But he doesn't really believe. He believes, perhaps, in an empty tomb, but not a resurrected body. True belief only comes when he understands the Scriptures.

It's striking then that in the next story Mary recognises Jesus not when she *sees* him, but when she *hears* him. Why? Because the Good Shepherd "calls his own sheep by name ... and his sheep follow him because they know his voice" (10 v 3-4).

Finally, John 20 ends with Jesus telling Thomas, "Because you have *seen* me, you have believed; blessed are those who have *not seen* and yet have believed" (20 v 29). John comments, "These [signs] are *written* that you may believe that Jesus is the Messiah, the Son of God, and that by believing you may have life in his name" (v 31).

You don't need to see the empty tomb or touch Christ's wounded side. True faith comes from *hearing* the Easter message. *You* can have resurrection faith. And if you do, then Jesus says to you, *My Father is your Father*, and John says, "You may have life in his name".

John picks up on this in his first letter:

That which was from the beginning, which we have heard, which we have seen with our eyes, which we have looked at and our hands have touched—this we proclaim concerning the Word of life. The life appeared; we have seen it and testify to it, and we proclaim to you the eternal life, which was with the Father and has appeared to us. We proclaim to you what we have seen and heard, so that you also may have fellowship with us. And our fellowship is with the Father and with his Son, Jesus Christ.   *(1 John 1 v 1-3)*

John surely has in mind the encounter with Thomas: heard, seen, touched. The apostles met the risen Jesus in the flesh, so they could proclaim to us the Word of life.

The sticking point is not the evidence. The sticking point is that, if we believe the evidence, then we must cry, "My Lord and my God". We need, as we've seen all along, to admit our need and submit our lives. And too often people prefer to doubt the evidence than bow to Jesus.

My Lord and my God. Will you say that to the risen Lord Jesus today?

Pray

O God, be present with us always, dwell within our hearts.
With your light and your Spirit
guide our souls, our thoughts, and all our actions,
that we may teach your Word,
that your healing power may be in us
and in your worldwide church. Amen.

Philip Melanchthon (1497-1560)

EASTER SUNDAY

John 20 v 1

The opening words of this chapter are a surprise—
even if our Easter traditions mean the surprise is
somewhat lost on us. Given all the talk of Jesus rising
after three days (such as John 2 v 20), we would have
expected John's Easter story to begin, "On the third
day…" But it begins on the *first day*.

We're meant, I think, to remember the opening words
of John's Gospel, which are themselves an echo of the
opening of the whole Bible story: "In the beginning…"
(Genesis 1 v 1 and John 1 v 1). John is telling the story
of creation and re-creation.

The story of creation begins in darkness, and then on
the first day God created light. John's Easter story like-
wise begins in darkness. "While it was still dark," he says
in 20 v 1. It echoes 13 v 30 when, as Judas left to begin
the process that ended in Jesus' crucifixion, we read,
"And it was night". Three days have passed since then,
but spiritually we're still in darkness. But everything is
about to burst into light. Just as in the story of creation
light replaces darkness on the first day, so in the story
of new creation light is going to replace darkness on the
first day.

Mary thinks Jesus is the gardener. It's clearly a mistake. But perhaps John points to a bigger truth. God gave Adam a garden to tend and extend. Yet humanity rebelled against God and brought a curse upon creation. But here is Jesus, the new Adam, humanity made new, ready to restore creation. The 5th-century theologian Jerome says, "When Mary Magdalene had seen the Lord and thought that he was the gardener ... she was mistaken, indeed, in her vision, but the very error had its prototype [that is, had an element of truth]. Truly, indeed, Jesus was the gardener of his paradise, of his trees of paradise" (Homily 87 on John 1 v 1-14).

This is probably also how we should read 20 v 22: "And with that he breathed on them and said, 'Receive the Holy Spirit'". It seems to be a symbolic act that looks forward to Pentecost. But it also recalls the creation of humanity, when God breathed his Spirit into an inert clay form and created a living soul (Genesis 2 v 7). Jesus is re-creating humanity, breathing new life by his Spirit.

So it's significant that the story ends with the words: "These are written that you may believe that Jesus is the Messiah, the Son of God, and that by believing you may have life in his name" (John 20 v 31).

How did God create? Through his word. How does God re-create? Through his word.

This, too, is how we should read verse 23: "If you forgive anyone's sins, their sins are forgiven; if you do not forgive them, they are not forgiven". The message of Easter is preached by God's people. Those who receive that message are forgiven; those who reject that message are not forgiven.

That's the message that comes to you now: the promise of forgiveness and life by believing in Jesus. If, along with Thomas, you say to him, "My Lord and my God", then today you stand as part of a re-created, eternal humanity. And this, surely, is reason to have a very happy Easter.

Meditate

The Son is the image of the invisible God,
the firstborn over all creation.
For in him all things were created:
things in heaven and on earth, visible and invisible,
whether thrones or powers or rulers or authorities;
all things have been created through him and for him.
He is before all things, and in him all things hold together.
And he is the head of the body, the church;
he is the beginning and the firstborn from among the dead,
so that in everything he might have the supremacy.
For God was pleased to have all his fullness dwell in him,
and through him to reconcile to himself all things,
whether things on earth or things in heaven,
by making peace through his blood, shed on the cross.

Colossians 1 v 15-20

HARDBACK DEVOTIONALS
FOR DAILY BIBLE READING

90 days with the Reformers in Genesis, Exodus, Psalms, and Galatians

Calvin, Luther, Bullinger & Cranmer

Open up the Bible with 90 devotions by famous Reformers including Luther and Calvin.
Edited by Dr Lee Gatiss.

Hardback | 288pp
ISBN: 9781784980863

90 Days in Ruth, Jeremiah, and 1 Corinthians

Mark Dever & Mike McKinley

Ninety days of open-Bible devotionals with Mark Dever and Mike McKinley. Includes space for journaling.

Hardback | 288pp
ISBN: 9781784981235

EXPLORE GOD'S WORD
EVERY DAY OF THE YEAR

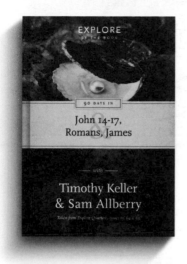

90 days in John 14–17, Romans, and James

Timothy Keller & Sam Allberry

Open up the Bible with 90 devotions by Timothy Keller and Sam Allberry. Includes space for journaling.

Hardback | 288pp
ISBN: 9781784981228

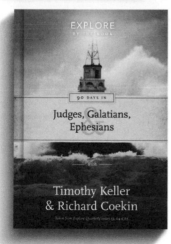

90 Days in Judges, Galatians, and Ephesians

Timothy Keller & Richard Coekin

Ninety days of open-Bible devotionals with Timothy Keller and Richard Coekin. Includes space for journaling.

Hardback | 288pp
ISBN: 9781784981631

thegoodbook
COMPANY

BIBLICAL | RELEVANT | ACCESSIBLE

At The Good Book Company, we are dedicated to helping Christians and local churches grow. We believe that God's growth process always starts with hearing clearly what he has said to us through his timeless word—the Bible.

Ever since we opened our doors in 1991, we have been striving to produce resources that honour God in the way the Bible is used. We have grown to become an international provider of user-friendly resources to the Christian community, with believers of all backgrounds and denominations using our Bible studies, books, evangelistic resources, DVD-based courses and training events.

We want to equip ordinary Christians to live for Christ day by day, and churches to grow in their knowledge of God, their love for one another, and the effectiveness of their outreach.

Call us for a discussion of your needs or visit one of our local websites for more information on the resources and services we provide.

Your friends at The Good Book Company

UK & EUROPE   thegoodbook.co.uk   0333 123 0880
NORTH AMERICA   thegoodbook.com   866 244 2165
AUSTRALIA   thegoodbook.com.au   (02) 9564 3555
NEW ZEALAND   thegoodbook.co.nz   (+64) 3 343 2463

WWW.CHRISTIANITYEXPLORED.ORG
Our partner site is a great place for those exploring the Christian faith, with a clear explanation of the good news, powerful testimonies and answers to difficult questions.